LOST
LAKE COUNTY
OHIO

LOST
LAKE COUNTY
OHIO

JENNIFER BORESZ ENGELKING

THE
History
PRESS

Published by The History Press
Charleston, SC
www.historypress.com

First published 2022

Manufactured in the United States

ISBN 9781467151313

Library of Congress Control Number: 2022936623

Notice: The information in this book is true and complete to the best of our knowledge. It is offered without guarantee on the part of the author or The History Press. The author and The History Press disclaim all liability in connection with the use of this book.

To my dear children,
I hope you always follow your dreams, treasure the stories of our past
and know how much you are loved.

With love always,
Mommy

CONTENTS

PREFACE

History exists in waves, flowing in and out of generations through stories and passed down through heirlooms. Some stories get told again and again, while others fade over time. We keep the pieces that mean the most, that remind us of who we are and where we come from. But along the way, some of the details are lost, stories are forgotten and the broken pieces discarded.

I watch my children's eyes light up when they hold a coin that once belonged to their great-great-grandpa or costume jewelry their great-grandma once wore, and it strikes me that they already understand that these aren't just objects but important pieces that bind us with our past, with the relatives who still teach and inspire us, even years after they are gone.

I wrote *Hidden History of Lake County, Ohio* to share the story behind the story of many of the places in Lake County that still exist in some form today, and as I researched, I discovered fascinating places and industries that are gone, which I'm thrilled to now share with you in *Lost Lake County, Ohio*.

We are a county built by hardworking pioneers and innovative businessmen and women, who created industries from nothing that allowed our cities to grow and thrive. We are uniquely situated on Lake Erie, which has positioned us to be an important piece of the puzzle in some of our country's most pivotal moments in history. Even the great tragedies and disasters of our county allow us to learn from our past.

But many of the historic documents that tell these stories are at risk of being lost. Photos are fading, and delicate papers are crumbling. The men and women who preserve our city archives in historical societies throughout Lake County understand the true value of our history and, thankfully, preserve it for future generations. They are the keepers of history, not just for one family but for our entire county.

My book is certainly not a complete chronological history of Lake County—there are many other wonderful books to fill that role—but, with the help of many dedicated archivists, historians and residents, it captures tales most at risk of being lost. These are stories that I hope you'll pass down to your children and even your children's children, just as you might pass down a treasured family heirloom. By sharing our precious Lake County history with future generations, we can hope that it will continue to be carried on, ebbing and flowing from generation to generation, like the waves of Lake Erie, reminding us of where we began, teaching us about what we've lost along the way and inspiring us to learn from the past, allowing it to guide us in the future.

ACKNOWLEDGEMENTS

I t takes a lot of people to create a book, and I'm thankful and feel so blessed for everyone who has helped me on this journey. I appreciate the hard work and talent of everyone at The History Press/Arcadia Publishing who have played a role in editing, designing, promoting and selling my book. I'm grateful for the opportunity to work with John Rodrigue, acquisitions editor, for a second time. Thank you for your support and quick responses to my many questions. You truly help simplify the whole publishing process! Thank you, also, to Zoe Ames, Crystal Murray, Mike Nieken, Katie Parry and Jenni Tyler.

Thank you to Marc Bona, fellow History Press author and writer at Cleveland.com, for tracking down archived *Plain Dealer* articles for me for my Willowick Country Club story.

I am so appreciative of the many historians, librarians and authors who are dedicating their time to preserving our history. Thank you to the following for sharing photos and/or stories with me: Jane Carle, Kirtland Public Library; Dianne Cross and Marjorie Shook, Madison Historical Society; Ann Dewald, Indian Museum of Lake County; Sarah Dykstra, Penfield House LLC; Alan Hitchcox and Pat Lewis, Willoughby Historical Society; Earnestine Jones, Lake County NAACP; Jack Kless, Perry Historical Society; Gale Lippucci, Willowick Public Library; Dan Maxson, Concord Township/ Stone Schoolhouse Museum; Tom Pescha, Painesville Railroad Museum; Nancymarie Phillips, *The Song of the Shepherdess*; Jewels Phraner, Carnegie Hero Fund; Angela Schmidt, Eastlake Historical Society/City Council;

Lee Silvi, Fairport Marine Museum and Lighthouse; J. Mark Souther, PhD, professor of history at Cleveland State University; Kathy Suglia, Wickliffe Historical Society; Lori Watson, Leroy Heritage Association; and Cathi Weber, Little Red Schoolhouse.

Thank you, also, to Barb Auvil; Andy Avram, Lake Metroparks; David Bukovec and Rudy's Quality Meats; Maria Carlone, Marino's Hair Design; Lynn Carlton; Cindy Channell-Kurzinger; Susan Clark; Art and Pat Cz Stafford; Brian Dickey; Marilyn Esposito; Mary Everette; Kim Hendrix Hurst; Jennifer Hood, Grand River Council president; Dennis Lawrence; Kristi Lockwood; Linda (Loxterman) Jones; Barbara McMahon and the Willo Beach Park Association; Catherine McManus; Mary Ann Podd Bukky; Mayor Richard Regovich, Willowick; Deanna and Fred Rowe; Karen Sendek; Bill Smith; Deb Sposit; Brad Sullivan; Katherine Harris Szerdy; Roger Tetzlaff; Rachel Vanek; Chad Wacha and Barnes & Noble in Mentor; Marie Wickman; and Doug Wilber and Joughin Hardware.

Thank you to the wonderful people at our local libraries and businesses who support me by sharing and/or selling my books and hosting talks and book signings!

Thank you to you, dear reader, for reading my books. Your interest and support mean so much to me and inspire me to keep researching and writing!

A heartfelt thank-you to my longtime friends, including Adrian Shaw, Kristin Petruziello, Heather Husted and Beth Cattell.

Most of all, a big thank-you to my family: to my brother, Mike Boresz, and Jenalyn Kustron; brother-in-law and sister-in-law, Mike and Korene Engelking; and my nieces and nephew for cheering me on! To my aunt Peggy (Landig) Zirbes, who formerly served as Lake County Historical Society's volunteer association president and helped inspire my love of history.

Thank you to my grandparents, John and Margaret Perusek and Wilbert and June Boresz, who always acted like the books I created for them as a kid were the best literature they'd ever read. (I miss you all and treasure our memories and the lessons you taught me.)

Thank you to my mother-in-law and father-in-law, Mary Ann and Dave Engelking, for your ongoing love and encouragement, and for never missing an opportunity to suggest my book to prospective readers.

Thank you to my parents, Joanne and Dale Boresz. I am a writer because of you. Thank you for encouraging my love of reading and imagination as a child, for helping me believe in myself as a teen, for continuing to inspire me to always go after my dreams as an adult and, through it all, for showing me constant love and support. And thank you, Dad, for the design and ongoing development of my website, www.jenniferboresz.com! I really appreciate it! I love you both!

Thank you to my husband and best friend, Brian, and our three amazing children. Thank you for being excited right along with me when I discover a new piece of a story (or when you see "Mom's book" when we're out and about), for believing in me every step of the way and for making me laugh and feel loved every day. I love you with all my heart!

Chapter 1

NATIVE AMERICANS AND PIONEERS

Lake County, Ohio, nestled along Lake Erie's north shore, is rich in history. Early inhabitants were drawn to the region for its beauty and plentiful resources, including forests for building; rivers and lakes for fishing, transporting goods and travel; and rich soil for growing crops.

The Paleo-Indians are believed to have been the first human inhabitants to arrive in Ohio, around 13,000 BC. Archaic man followed and then, eventually, the Mound Builders, a highly developed society that grew crops and made tools and weapons, often found inside the animal-shaped mounds they built.

Mounds have been found throughout Lake County, but most were leveled by farmers settling the region. According to Ann L. Dewald, longtime director of the Indian Museum of Lake County, in Mentor, mounds once existed in several Lake County Metroparks, including Chagrin River Park, where a dig took place in the 1970s on a mound believed to have been used for ceremonial purposes, but it's unclear whether that mound exists today. Mounds can still be found on private property throughout Lake County.

Whittlesey Tradition

The people of the Whittlesey (pronounced Whittle-see) Tradition lived in Lake County from about AD 900 to 1650 and were named after geologist

Postcard of the Chagrin River, Willoughby. *Author's collection.*

and antiquarian Colonel Charles Whittlesey. He was interested in how they lived and explored their sites throughout Ohio, including remains of villages near the lakeshore and on ridgetops overlooking major river valleys.

Ann Dewald, director of the Indian Museum of Lake County, says that the Whittlesey generally lived close to rivers and occupied a wedge-shaped area from the north at the New York/Pennsylvania line to as far south as Youngstown. "They knew every little stream. They knew streams that only existed in the spring. They knew about all of them," she explains. "If you're really hunting for artifacts, you find the streams and that's where you walk."

Searching for Indian artifacts is a popular childhood pastime in Lake County (I remember digging in the yard with my brother, Mike, and our neighbors, hoping the rocks we found might just be arrowheads). Many people have discovered prehistoric artifacts on their own property, like Fred Gehri of Mentor, who found them while plowing his fields near Garfield Road, from 1910 to 1913.

For years, people thought those artifacts came from the Erie Indians, but Dewald says the Eries never actually lived in Lake County, and several indicators of the artifacts' true origins can be found in carving and pottery-making methods. Whittlesey made their arrows as little triangles without indentations and, before that, with little notches. Dewald says people didn't

Fred Gehri of Mentor plowing his fields near Garfield Road, where he found prehistoric artifacts from 1910 to 1913. *Courtesy of Indian Museum of Lake County.*

innovate in pottery making. "If you made pottery, you made it like your mother and grandmother and didn't deviate."

Several decades ago, when an archaeologist went to Erie, Pennsylvania, where the Erie Indians were known to live, she noticed their pottery looked different than what we have here. It's been thirty-five years since the museum stopped saying Erie Indians were in the area, but Dewald says some people still won't accept it.

REEVES VILLAGE SITE

One of the county's most important Whittlesey sites was the Reeves Village Site, about one-quarter mile south of the mouth of the Chagrin River (called "Shagrin" by Native Americans, meaning "clear water"). It was across the street from Eastlake Middle School, under what is now the Marina Park Condominiums.

The site was made of two walls of earth enclosing an area at the edge of the river bluff, according to the local history book *Here Is Ohio's Lake County,* written and compiled by members of the Lake County Historical Society. Many artifacts were found at the site, including knives, drills, arrowheads and

Indian artifacts found at Reeves Road Site. *Courtesy of Indian Museum of Lake County.*

spearheads and a large assortment of smoking pipes (now on display at the Indian Museum of Lake County), including one made of a brachiopod fossil.

Ann Dewald says that the buried Indian village once sat on farmland. When the property was sold to a condo developer, the public was given several weeks to dig at the site before construction began. That's how the museum got its start, with an abundance of artifacts found during that dig.

So far, the gravesites of the people who lived in that village have not been found.

FAIRPORT VILLAGE SITE

Another major Whittlesey site is in Fairport, about three-quarters of a mile from Lake Erie, south of the railroad crossing on East Street (at the baseball diamonds.) High school students discovered the site and helped with the dig in the 1930s. Ann Dewald says Fairport High School used to have a room filled with artifacts from the dig, but no one is sure where they went.

Fairport High School students at excavation dig at Fairport Village Site. *Courtesy of Indian Museum of Lake County.*

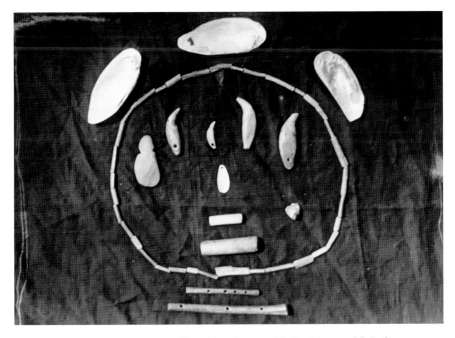

Indian artifacts found at Fairport Village Site. *Courtesy of Indian Museum of Lake County.*

Grantham Site

Shaunungas was one of the major villages located on the Grand River, called "Geauga" or "Sheauga shipe" by Native Americans, names that are believed to mean "racoon river." (The French later named it LaGrande Riviere.)

Thousands of items, including storage pots, arrowheads and chisels, have been found at the edge of a bluff overlooking the Grand River valley. Burials linked to the village were found at 1200 East Street in Fairport, at Grantham Inc. Painesville historian Bill Smith recalls seeing tents at the excavation site, across the street from the Lake Metroparks Grand River Landing sign.

Ann Dewald discovered a July 29, 1985 *Painesville Gazette* article in the archives of the Indian Museum of Lake County with the headline "Indian Skeletons Uncovered." It states that a bulldozer unearthed the remains when property owner John P. Grantham wanted to put in a fly ash pit. Dewald heard that the coroner was called, but they laughed, saying, "I'm hundreds of years too late; you need to call an archaeologist."

The remains of 115 Indians were found. They weren't buried with much, but one Indian had a quiver of arrows. The article says Grantham wanted the remains to be returned to the site; however, it's unknown if they were.

Dewald says there are Indian campsites throughout Lake County, including the Andrews Osborne School property, in Willoughby, where several digs have taken place. "It's astounding how much there really is, but they had thousands of years to put it there. It was a wonderful place for these people because they had a wealth of food. They had Lake Erie, so they had plenty of animals. At one point, there were buffalo here, so even large animals. It was a good place to live."

Indian Point Park

Two rows of mounds that meet at a point with steep cliffs leading down to Paine Creek and the Grand River on either side can be found at Lake Metroparks Indian Point Park, in Leroy Township.

As one of the earliest architectural works in the region, it's listed on the National Register of Historic Places by the National Park Service. One historical marker at the site says the Whittlesey dwellings were rectangular or oval-shaped and made from saplings and tree bark. Another reads, "There is evidence that the walls were built B.C. and the site was occupied again

Wissalohichan cadets on Indian Point in 1912. *Courtesy of Leroy Heritage Association.*

around 1500 A.D. by the Whittlesey Tradition people. It is uncertain if the site was a village or was used as a ceremonial center. After 1650 A.D. the area became a neutral hunting ground for various historic tribes."

According to Ann Dewald, in between the mounds are manmade basins, guiding rainwater down, each one a little lower than the next so the water didn't erode the edges. She thinks women and children were put up top, to keep them safe from the Seneca (part of the Iroquois, known to kill anyone they came across, who came to the area from New York to hunt in the spring and fall).

There were fewer Whittlesey, and it's unknown whether they were more peaceful, but they eventually disappeared from the area, with no indication that they joined another group, leading experts to believe many were killed.

Charles A. Lyman, who bought several acres at Indian Point, found arrowheads, spearpoints, pipes and even a skeleton. From 1878 to 1918, the land was used as a military camp for high school boys, known as Lymans Camp Wissalohichan, with many cadets going on to fight in World War I. When a cadet completed two years of camp, their name was carved into a totem stone. (Many of the campers' names can still be seen on it today, along the trail near the point.)

Later, the site became a Finnish camp, Kaleva Lodge, and a stone hut was built and used as a sauna, remaining intact until the 1970s.

BIG WATER GOD

Native Americans believed several areas were sacred in Lake County, like Little Mountain, where legend says the Great Spirit lived among the springs, caves and rock formations.

The Big Water God was believed to be present at the ever-bubbling gas spring in Lake Erie, offshore from today's Perry Nuclear Power Plant. The spring was two to three rods inland from the shoreline, according to members of the early surveying parties, and was filled with fish, which Native Americans regarded as a special gift of the god when he was in a good humor.

The bubbling gas spring can still be seen today and is a popular fishing spot.

PERRY INDIAN BURIAL SITES

Indian relics have been found throughout Perry, in the woods, on farms, and in nursery fields.

"The Indian trail followed South Ridge Road that marked the high-water point of Lake Erie thousands of years ago. At the corner of South Ridge and Lane Roads in Perry there is evidence of an Indian burial site," according to Mary Platko's *A Little Bit of Perry History*. In about 1919, the South Church was moved off the cemetery lot at that corner, and when digging the foundation for the new location of the building, diagonally across from the cemetery, an Indian graveyard was discovered. "The remains of nine Indians were found there together with flint spearheads, tomahawk heads of stone, flint arrowheads and skin feathers and scrapers."

Many people think of Lake Erie as being the only lake bordering the county, but it's the smallest of five to seven lakes that shrank as glaciers melted and receded about nineteen thousand years ago. Lake Warren was the first and biggest, emptying out through the Ohio River. Sometimes the ice blocked water from going east, and some lakes stretched nearly to the far edge of Michigan. Ann Dewald says that Route 20, Middle Ridge and South Ridge were all different lake banks, and Native Americans used them as trails because they were the easiest place to walk.

PERRY'S AMERICAN INDIAN PRINCESS

For many years, on Memorial Day, a mystery lady arrived in Cleveland's oldest cemetery on Erie Street, sprinkling corn and decorating the grave of Joc-o-Sot, a Sauk chief who died in 1844. In the 1950s, newspaper articles were published asking the public to help identify her, and reporters sometimes waited for her in the cemetery.

In 1961, Wanda Palmer called the *Cleveland Press* to tell them the mystery lady was her sister, Princess Mahoniaee Au Paw Chee Kaw Paw Qua Keokuk of Perry, Ohio. The surname of Palmer was given to her family by the government, but according to *A Little Bit of Perry History*, she was known in Perry as Mona Cline or Mahonia.

Her grandfather Chief Thunderwater Henry Palmer, titular head of the supreme council of Indian tribes of the United States and Canada, raised her in Cleveland. He was a well-known medicine man, selling Mohawk Penetrating Oil and Thunderwater's Tonic Bitters. His Indian name was Oghema Niagara, since he was born and christened in an Indian ritual near Niagara Falls, where he took Mahonia to be christened when she was eleven. While they were there, a Protestant minister also gave her a Christian baptism. "Grandpa Chief," as she called him, vowed to return with her on her seventeenth birthday so she could choose between paganism and Christianity. She chose to follow her mother's Christian religion but continued to carry on Indian traditions such as visiting, and caring for, the graves of her ancestors.

In the late 1950s, Mona moved to Townline Road in Perry Township, and she owned a nursing home on Route 20, later demolished to make way for the Perry Nuclear Power Plant. She died at the age of seventy-five and is buried in the Perry Cemetery. Since she never had any children, one of Mona's nieces carried on the tradition of caring for the graves.

EARLY PIONEERS

Although Native Americans first occupied the land, the French followed; they built a trading post called Charlton at the mouth of the Chagrin River as early as 1750 but left the area after being defeated in the French and Indian War.

In 1783, the Treaty of Paris ended the American Revolutionary War, and the British Crown ceded most of its territory east of the Mississippi River to the United States, doubling the country's size and paving the way for western expansion.

In 1794, Native Americans were defeated by the American army encroaching on their land in the Battle of Fallen Timbers, in Maumee (near Toledo). This led several tribes to sign the Treaty of Greenville, giving their land to the government and relocating to northwestern Ohio.

States were encouraged to give up their claims to their western lands after the Revolutionary War to create the Northwest Territory, which became Connecticut's Western Reserve, which would be sold to finance the newly independent country.

In 1796, surveyor Charles Parker, with the Connecticut Land Company, built his cabin (possibly the first house in Willoughby Township) and several huts at the mouth of the Chagrin River.

The Connecticut Land Company was formed by a group of investors who bought more than three million acres of land at forty cents an acre. In the spring of 1796, with Moses Cleaveland (the city of Cleveland's namesake) as director, the fifty-one surveyors headed west to check their assets and establish north–south range lines sectioned into five-square-mile townships so the land could be sold. They encountered many hardships and returned east in the fall with expertly drafted survey maps. When another group arrived to complete the survey in 1797, they discovered their territorial holdings were only two-and-a-half million instead of three million acres, because the rest was under Lake Erie.

The surveyors and early pioneers quickly realized what the Indians knew all along: that the land was filled with great promise. The Connecticut Land Company began setting up offices in the Western Reserve and promoting sales. Many of the property lines they created are the basis for today's deeds, including original range, township and tract designations.

Grand River also provided entry into the Western Reserve for many settlers, including Connecticut Land agent Turhand Kirtland, who arrived at the mouth of the river in 1798. He became a large landholder in Kirtland Township, which was named after him.

Christopher G. Crary arrived in Kirtland Township when he was five years old with his parents and siblings, who left Massachusetts in May 1811. According to Anne B. Prusha's *History of Kirtland, Ohio*, they were the first permanent settlers. Crary's home in Kirtland was on a knoll cleared by his father, about a mile west of Chillicothe Road. He recalled his family's trip from Mentor to Kirtland:

We took the Old Chillicothe Road, which had been traversed scarcely at all, except by cattle and wild beasts. The trees on either side were so interlaced as to form a canopy overhead, which rendered it quite romantic, but gloomy. We forded the Chagrin without difficulty and supposed our worst fears closing around us.

They walked the rest of the way, carrying lighted torches to ward off bears and wolves. Chillicothe Road was one of the first and most important roads into the Western Reserve, running from Painesville through Mentor to the Kirtland Flats, where it crossed the East Branch of the Chagrin River and continued down to Chillicothe, which was the capital of the state.

Crary recalls that the first Kirtland school began in a private home in the Flats, around 1813. His sister, Estella, was a teacher who was paid fifty cents a week and board, staying with each family whose children attended school. Crary describes school breakfast as johnnycake (a cornmeal flatbread that resembles a pancake), boiled potatoes, fried pork, grease and sometimes butter. For lunch, choices were only cold johnnycake or cold potatoes. Then dinner included johnnycake or potatoes with milk, all served without salt because it was too expensive and scarce.

By 1818, a log schoolhouse was built in Kirtland, with a frame school built the following year, and Estella was paid twenty-five cents a day to teach a dozen students.

Chapter 2

EARLY INDUSTRY

1700s–1800s

Industry began in the cabins of the earliest settlers, where men crafted wooden bowls, pitchforks and brooms, while women made material for clothing and bedding, cooked and preserved food.

Lillie Tryon Curtis, born in 1856, wrote down some of her recollections of growing up in Waite Hill, which were published in the 1978 *Lake County Historical Society Quarterly*. She wrote that only brown sugar was available when she was a child because block sugar was unknown. Loaf sugar came in large cones, broken apart by using a wooden mallet.

"Raisins came in clusters, and required stemming, seeding, washing, spreading, and drying before they could be used—it took two days to make a fruit cake. Corn-starch was as yet unknown—sago, arrow-root [*sic*] and isinglass or tapioca were used instead."

Curtis said all women made preserves, but there were no "lighting jars" or "self-scalers" in those days, so preserving took a long time. "The hot jar was sealed by filling in the groove around the cover with a hot cement made of resin and beeswax, kneaded with the fingers until the taffy-like coil was ready to be pressed into place. Great skill and much experience were necessary to assure success. But still, there were always delicious jams and preserves, marmalades and apple-butters, applesauce, and pickles to depend upon."

She said by 1930, most of what was produced on farms and in homes could be bought in the store. "'Men worked from sun to sun, and woman's work was never done'—but there was a joy in that work, a family togetherness that the convenience of the corner store cannot replace."

Postcard of bridge in Waite Hill. *Author's collection.*

The first industry outside the cabin was the gristmill, which consisted of a large grindstone rotating over a stationary stone, while wheat was poured between them, to produce a sifted flour.

According to *Here Is Ohio's Lake County,* "Power for the early mills varied. In Harpersfield, animals were used to turn the grindstone. Madison's Abel Kimball operated a wind-driven wheel. Most popular of all was water-power, a familiar idea brought overseas by the Pilgrims."

Two types of waterwheels were used by the early nineteenth century: the overshot wheel (known to be more efficient), built at a natural waterfall or dam using the water's force and weight falling on the wheel to turn the shaft, and the undershot wheel, built at stream level, using only the water's force.

Chagrin Mills/Eastlake

New England lawyer David Abbott was the first permanent settler in Chagrin Mills, arriving in the summer of 1797 after hearing of great opportunities in a vast unexplored territory known as Ohio, which would achieve statehood in 1803. He left his job and family behind, built a boat and headed west. When he arrived, he stopped in Charlton, at the mouth of the Chagrin River, chose a parcel of land and traveled back to Connecticut to finalize the purchase. He built his settlement, later known as Abbotts Mill or Abbotstown, on the east bank of the river at the site of an Indian village.

Abbott learned the Connecticut Land Company was offering $200, or a $500 loan at 6 percent interest, to anyone willing to build the first gristmill, so he built a water-powered mill along the western bank of the Chagrin River, about two miles south of Lake Erie. In 1798, it became the first gristmill on record in Lake County; it is believed to have been at the intersection of the northeast channel with the west branch of the Chagrin. However, in 1803, high water forced Abbott to rebuild two miles up the river near the ford at Erie and Pelton Roads.

Abbot also became a civic leader and builder of the first sizable schooner (twenty tons) in the Western Reserve, the *Cuyahoga Packet*, which sailed Lake Erie until 1812, when it was captured by the British.

Willoughby alone had seven mills in the 1800s.

BOYCE MILL

Boyce Mill was built on Erie Street and Pelton Road (known as Mill Hill) in Willoughby. "It does a fine business in both custom and merchant grinding. The waters of the Chagrin river furnish the motive-power," reads *History of Geauga and Lake Counties, Ohio, 1798–1878.*

The mill, originally opened under different ownership, was transferred to Julia French Boyce, who was married to Joseph Boyce in 1882, and it operated until May 17, 1893, when it was destroyed by a flood. After three days of heavy rain, the mill was swept from its foundation and hurled against the Chagrin River bridge. It was never rebuilt because other modes of power had become more economical.

According to the Willoughby Historical Society, in the spring of 1913, Willoughby had another damaging flood. Trees were carried downstream, roads were impassable and bridges were washed out. At one point, below the Gilson farm, the river was nearly a mile wide, and water flooded the boiler room at the American Clay Machinery Company.

Other gristmills once existed in Lake County, including Jordan's mill in Concord Township, Trumbull's mill in south Madison on the Grand River,

The Old Boyce Mill in Willoughby. *Courtesy of Willoughby Historical Society.*

Lost Nation Road Bridge looking east during the 1913 flood. *Courtesy of Willoughby Historical Society.*

Eli Bond's in Perry, James Ford's on Arcola Creek in north Madison, William Judd's on the Chagrin River and even Little Marsh Creek in Mentor.

Many water-powered sawmills were near gristmills or combined both operations, like Abbott's. Benjamin Bates built a saw/gristmill in Leroy Township by 1816, and Hendrick Paine built his mill in Paine's Hollow.

WAITE HILL PAIL FACTORY/KIRTLAND MILLS

In 1930, Lillie Tryon Curtis recalled the hills and ravines in Waite Hill in the 1800s and their crystal-clear springs, "free from mineral taste and delicious."

Curtis said that the rolling hills, between the ravines, were a haven for children. A gully emerged from the woods, spreading into a marsh that led into the river below, and a treeless pasture, called Bousfield Lot after English settler John Bousfield, overlooked the Markell Valley. At the foot of the steep hillside stood Bousfield's pail and tub factory.

> *This factory had by 1860 been abandoned for several years but, I think, when in operation, had been run by water from our big spring, conveyed by flume to an over-shot wheel....On our side, a road climbed a hill and met the Waite Hill road* [sic] *at the corner, making at the same place a sharp angle with the Kirtland road. These were the roads by which the Bousfield pails and tubs were brought to the people of the Hill and the country to the south and east of us. After Mr. Bousfield left, Charles Fessenden and Nelson Waite operated the mill for a short while manufacturing washing-machines, but after not too many years the mill was altogether abandoned. After that, it remained for many years the chief center of "pernicious activity" for the idle boys of Kirtland Flats.*

According to Anne B. Prusha's *A History of Kirtland, Ohio*, Kirtlanders were an enterprising bunch who established mills to provide food and lumber for the community. Because of the waterpower the East Branch of the Chagrin provided, industry and economic life were centered primarily over the Flats. Even the post office was named Kirtland Mills.

In 1816, Grandison Newell visited Kirtland on a trading trip to Ohio and enjoyed it so much he bought several lots and brought his family back. He started out as a farmer, but soon added a "pocket furnace" to his log cabin, scraping bog iron from the surface of the ground to feed it, which allowed him to produce the first cast-iron plows in the Western Reserve. (Bog iron has been found in recent years in Holden Arboretum, near the site of the furnace.)

By 1829, a lathe and chair factory had been built on the north bank of the Chagrin, with a second building, powered by water, on the south bank.

Newell K. Whitney set up the first store in Kirtland in 1823, and a year later, he built a distillery across the river on the Flats, to turn the extra grain into whiskey. According to *Here Is Ohio's Lake County*,

> *This was a usable product which could be both stored and transported much more conveniently than grain. Whiskey was commonly used as a medium of exchange in the early days. Even schoolteachers and ministers received part of their pay in a jug of whiskey, and all the neighbors gathered for a barn-raising or harvest, expected a generous supply to cheer their efforts.*

At first, Kirtland residents thought the distillery would benefit the young town, bringing in business while providing a source of yeast to make bread. According to Crary,

> *Juveniles were highly pleased with the prospects before us. We could have our half acre of corn all to ourselves and have a ready market and through the Still House we saw visions of boughten suspenders, sleeve buttons, handkerchiefs, and possibly soft shirts instead of tow linen. Haying and harvesting could not be done without it....Making sugar, gathering sap in stormy weather and boiling nights required whiskey.*

During the fourteen years the distillery operated, three workers died young, one was found dead with a jug and another, while drunk, froze his feet and legs, which affected him his whole life. Even the proprietor, Warren Corning, lost his son to alcoholism.

The milldam also had connections to the Mormon community at the nearby Kirtland Temple. Karl Ricks Anderson's *Joseph Smith's Kirtland Eyewitness Accounts* reads:

> *Most of the baptisms were performed in the Chagrin River in a large pool created where the river was dammed to provide power for the grist mill. One of the most "chilling" baptisms was that of Dr. Willard Richards, a physician from Massachusetts, who was baptized by his cousin Brigham Young on December 31, 1836. Heber C. Kimball and others spent the afternoon in cutting the ice to prepare for the baptism.*

Postcard of the milldam in Kirtland, Ohio. *Author's collection.*

James E. Naughton writes in *70 Years of Living in Kirtland,*

> *The dam was on Overlook Drive and owned by Millie Brewster who, the story goes, blew up the dam because she didn't like the young folks skinny dipping….It was still a great swimming hole and we Kirtland High School students in the fall and spring would go down and swim at lunch time.*

ABBOTT'S MILL, PAINESVILLE

Abbott's Mill in Painesville (unrelated to the one in Willoughby) operated on the west bank of the Grand River, near present-day Recreation Park, from the 1860s through 1958, when it was destroyed in a fire. At least two other mills were at the site, known as Painesville Mills, before Abbott's.

A May 6, 1886 *Painesville Telegraph* article says that in 1806, Joel Scott and his four sons settled at Skinner Farm on the Grand River and built a sawmill that operated for nearly two decades, establishing a shipyard on the flats below where they built two schooners: the *Champion* and the *Farmer.*

In 1826, the Scotts, busy with other enterprises, transferred the property to the Geauga Furnace Company. Soon after, the mill burned, but an even better one was built. It changed hands several times, warehouses were built to hold grain and farmers brought their wool to have it carded into rolls at the carding mill built below.

The mill burned a second time in 1859 and was rebuilt once again. In April 1866, the dam was swept away by floods, but every piece of hewn white oak timber was recovered along the river and lakeshore and was used in reconstructing the seemingly indestructible mill.

By 1870, S. Bigler had purchased the property, but several years later, the dam was left dry when high water cut through the road east of the bridge and made a new channel for the river. The water supply became unreliable, so Bigler introduced steam power. He became partners with his son, Frank S. Bigler, and A.H. Noble of the Diamond Mills in Youngstown.

The mill's reputation for quality flour, produced from wheat from neighboring farms, grew, and the flour was shipped to cities beyond Painesville. The mill was also known for making buckwheat flour as white as wheat flour, using a patented machine that removed the black hulls from the grain.

The King Bridge Company built a bridge at the site in 1896, which was torn down in 1986 and replaced by the current bridge.

Postcard of Abbott's Mill and Dam in Painesville. *Courtesy of Rachel Vanek, from the collection of Joseph and Betty Koelliker Jr.*

The mill is often referred to as Abbott's Mill, after Eugene A. Abbott, whose father bought the mill from Bigler in 1904. It was located on the north side of the Main Street bridge and fell into disrepair and burned in the 1950s. When the present bridge was constructed, the remains of the dam and mill foundation were removed.

Paine's Hollow

In 1818, Paine's Hollow in Leroy Township was a little valley settled by Hendrick E. Paine (nephew of Edward Paine, founder of Painesville), who built a log cabin on a terrace next to the falls. His granddaughter, Mary Paine Kewish, wrote in *A Bit of Pioneer History*, "The uniform logs for the house were notched near the ends and rolled up one above another into a square, the notched ends interlocking and holding the whole together. The roof was a split log roof with no shingles; earth provided a floor for the cabin."

Hendrick Paine and his family made a seven-mile journey from Painesville that took all day, passing through the Huntoon settlement at Ohio Route 86 and Williams Road in Concord, through Carter's Corners at Carter and Vrooman and into the valley from the south, crossing the creek above the falls. Mrs. Paine carried her child while riding a horse; the family brought a team of oxen and three heavily loaded wagons. "They ventured into the wilderness to take advantage of nature's gift, waterpower. The water at Paine's Hollow plunged over a rocky ledge, making a sheer fall of 23 feet before it reached the basin below."

Samuel Phelps, of Painesville, designed and furnished the sawmill, with a frame raised and hauled from Martin's Mill in Concord and a bridge across the creek.

"Homes and businesses began to spring up all around the falls, and in 1826, with capital from Phelps, Paine built an iron forge and furnace," said Lori Watson, treasurer and historian of the Leroy Heritage Association. "Before long there was a gristmill, a blacksmith shop, a shoemaker, a tannery, an ashery, a wagon shop and more."

By 1836, fifty-one students were attending a newly built school, and the mill was running nonstop, Monday through Saturday night. By 1842, there were forty-seven buildings and homes in the area.

Watson explained, "Paine's sawmill made wood shingles. The ashery converted hardwood ashes to lye and potash, which were used to make soap,

Paine's Sawmill
Paine Hollow
Leroy Township

Paine's Sawmill at Paine's Hollow in Leroy Township. *Courtesy of the Leroy Heritage Association.*

tanned leather and glass. Iron ore from the bogs in Madison was hauled to Leroy and converted to pig iron. The forge at Pain Hollow produced farm implements, tools and household items for pioneers from here to Buffalo, New York."

By 1850, 1,100 people lived in Leroy and depended on the waterpower of the falls. However, the industrial boom didn't last. The hollow was stripped of trees (used to produce iron) and vegetation, which held the spring rains and fed the creek.

Watson said, "There was heavy flooding in the spring but not enough water in the creek during the summer months to turn the waterwheels. The mill and forge were both closed by 1859, and Leroy became a ghost town. Luckily, time and nature have restored the region's beauty."

Decades later, a ghost story was linked to Paine's Hollow. An article in the October 19, 1922 *Chillicothe Gazette* reads, "Lake County people are watching the trial of Frank Larman [later spelled Lerman] of Cleveland, in local courts on charge of second-degree murder, with interest perhaps unrivaled in the history of the county. By it, they recall to mind an incident that will, they say, become part of the community's legendary history."

Seven years earlier, Lerman owned a farm at Paine's Hollow when his handyman Harry Kipenstock (Henry Lipenstick) disappeared. The farm changed hands several times until Carl Logies bought it.

According to the *Chillicothe Gazette*, "Logies asserted that night after night, about 9:30, as he approached the barn where he kept his cattle, he saw 'something white' slip past it. He said the mysterious thing always disappeared in the direction of the well and gradually he claims [the] conviction came upon him that the well had something to do with the mystery."

One night, he heard his dog barking outside. When the barks changed to a whine of terror, he rushed out and saw a white mist hovering over a well across the road.

When he could no longer stand the nightly event, he decided to clean out the well (which had been filled with rocks) and made a grisly discovery, pulling out a half-rotted shoe containing bones. He immediately called the sheriff, and when county officials arrived, they discovered the remains of a battered man and a watch with a peculiar ruby charm, which helped identify the body as that of Henry Lipenstick. The watch had stopped at 9:35, the same hour Logies said the spirit roamed around.

Lerman was arrested a day later, an hour after the body of Lipenstick was buried in an unmarked grave in the cemetery.

"Since the body has been buried farmers claim the spirit of Paine's Hollow is at rest."

THE MADISON WHEEL COMPANY

The Madison Wheel Company had a large factory east of Lake Street along the north side of the railroad in 1881.

According to *Madison*, by Denise Michaud and the Madison Historical Society, the company manufactured wooden spoked wheels and supplied gears, axles, poles, shafts, bodies, tops and cushions, specializing in automobile wheels and bike, wagon and cushion tire wheels.

A 1902 advertisement in the *Blacksmith and Wheelwright Magazine* reads, "Our prices are so uniformly low that the temptation to use an inferior article is removed."

At its peak, the factory had several large frame buildings and employed sixty-five men. It closed in 1914 and was torn down in 1941.

Old Wheel Shop in Madison, October 5, 1884. *Courtesy of Madison Historical Society.*

IRON ORE

Iron ore, the source of much of Lake County's early industrial growth, was first discovered in 1812 in the swamps near North Ridge Road in Madison, with shallow pockets along the north ridge in Perry and south ridge in Concord, Leroy, Madison and Mentor.

The yellowish-brown ore, found in separate nodules or sheets, had a spongy texture. It was dug by hand and roasted in kilns with wood before being put into a furnace. "The ore of this area usually gave a yield of 25% to 35% iron. It was mixed with small amounts of phosphorous and manganese which gave an alloy of excellent quality. These two extra minerals gave pig iron strength and hardness, a material well suited for foundry work," reads *Here Is Ohio's Lake County*.

Early blast furnaces, made of brick and stone, had a stack about thirty-two feet high. Furnaces sat at the foot of a hillside and were loaded at the top by standing on a bridge on the bank. Layers of ore, charcoal and limestone, the fluxing agent, were dumped into the stack, and air, which increased the burning, was forced in by water-powered blowing machines.

Each day, the waste, or slag, was drawn off and a hole was drilled through the clay plug to release the molten slag. As explained in *Here Is Ohio's Lake County*, "Molten iron rushed from the furnace into troughs to form sow bars (pig iron) or was poured into molds to produce the desired shape of cast iron."

Men hauled in raw materials and took turns tending the kilns and furnaces, keeping them operating seven days a week. At their peak, the furnaces employed many residents and produced thirty-five tons of iron a week, providing households and farms with cheap iron products and bringing new money to the region through exports.

A Little Bit of Perry History says,

> *There were two railroad tracts leading from the top of the hill to the blast furnace. At the top of the hill was a pulley with a rope that was tied to a car for each set of rails. One car would be loaded with charcoal and limestone. When that car went down the hill, the rope pulled the empty car to the top of the hill, which then was loaded with bog iron ore and, in turn, pulled the other car up again.*

The first furnace in Lake County was likely in Mentor Township, near the intersection of Chillicothe and Little Mountain Roads. It manufactured

Postcard of Blair Covered Bridge, which was located on Blair Road, Perry Township. It was a 150-foot-long Howe truss bridge that spanned the Grand River from the 1860s to 1961, when it was replaced by a cement bridge. *Author's collection.*

cast-iron plows (the first made in the Reserve) and cast-iron bells. The Geauga Iron Company, founded in 1825 at Pepoon's Crossing (now Route 20) on the Grand River, was the longest-running furnace in Lake County's iron industry, closing in about 1870.

In 1825, several more furnaces began in Lake County: the Incorporate Company in Concord, Thorndike and Drury's in Perry, Wheeler's Erie Furnace in Madison and the Blair Furnace, at the bottom of Blair Road Hill in Perry. The Blair Bridge was the last covered (public) bridge in Lake County; it was built in 1866 at the site of the Blair Furnace and replaced in 1952.

Chapter 3

MARITIME HISTORY

Red skies at night, sailor's delight.
Red skies in the morning, sailor's warning.
—Old maritime saying

MADISON DOCK/ELLENSBURGH

It was known by many names—Arcole, Ellensburgh, Harper's Landing and Madison Dock—but the once-bustling town, at Dock Road and Lakeshore Boulevard along Arcola Creek, no longer exists today.

According to *Here Is Ohio's Lake County*, "In 1828, Samuel Wilkeson of Buffalo, New York, and Uri Seeley of Painesville purchased the Erie Furnace, renamed it after Wilkeson's Buffalo firm, Arcole, and incorporated the company with a capital stock of $100,000. Seeley was a prosperous farmer, widely known for his energy, integrity and activity in community affairs."

Wilkeson was a Pittsburgh salt merchant, carrying on trade as far as Lake Erie. He went into canal boating when the Erie Canal opened in 1825 and became determined to make Buffalo the leading port on Lake Erie. He was hoping Arcole Iron Company would stimulate shipping of manufacturing goods in and out of Buffalo.

Arcole was the most prosperous of our furnaces and one of the largest in the state. In 1839, it exported 1,400 tons of pig iron, said to be of excellent quality. For nearly two decades, it was the center of a flourishing community, producing stoves, hollowware (metal tableware, bowls, pitchers and teapots) and potash kettles.

The blue slag rocks the furnace produced can still be found locally, decorating gardens or even used in jewelry making.

As the demand to transport goods on Lake Erie increased, shipbuilding grew in Richmond and Fairport, and crafts of various sizes were constructed on the beaches of Mentor Headlands and Perry. However, Ellensburgh, at the mouth of Arcola Creek, is believed to have produced more ships than any other site.

When the Erie Canal opened, a man named Fuller built an entire steamboat himself at the site, shaping the timbers and forging the spikes and engine parts. It was the first steamboat built west of Buffalo and the third such ship on Lake Erie.

Ellensburgh was an active harbor for many years. The long deck built out into the lake was used by ships bringing limestone from Kelley's Island for Arcole Iron Company and ships sailing to Buffalo with Arcole products.

It was a common sight to see two- or three-masted schooners or single-deck shallow cargo vessels sailing past the dock out into the open lake.

To accommodate the many sailors and shipbuilders and the two thousand men employed by Arcole Iron Company, a three-story hotel stood about two hundred feet back from the shore near Dock Road, where the shout and songs of sailors were said to be heard far into the night.

A lighthouse keeper, who tended one lighthouse on the lakeshore by the creek and another at the end of the pier, lived across from the hotel. Other stores existed in the area, like Joel T. Norton's cabinet shop, which crafted sails for the ships and other ship furnishings.

The Arcole company store, located at the end of Dock Road, used due bills as money for the many workers who lived in the over two hundred log cabins and frame houses surrounding the furnace and on nearby farms.

THE DIAMOND ALKALI COMPANY

In Fairport, the docks were a busy industry for many years, as large freighters brought in loads of iron ore from mines in Minnesota and Michigan, which were transferred to local steel mills. In 1831, the docks were the first federally sponsored port facility on Lake Erie; fishing, shipbuilding and transporting goods helped make the port a success.

Diamond Alkali. *Photo courtesy of Kristi Lockwood, from the personal collection of George and Garnet Saari.*

The docks were the main employer until the untapped mineral resource of salt, lying deep under Lake Erie's shoreline, attracted Diamond Alkali. Construction of the Painesville plant, which would produce soda ash used in the manufacture of glass, began in 1911. Painesville was chosen because it could be reached by lake freighters bringing limestone from Michigan and railroads hauling coal from West Virginia.

Business boomed during World War I when the demand for glass increased. In 1920, the plant began manufacturing soda ash, caustic ash, laundry soda, soda crystal, bichromates, cement, chlorine alkalis and coke. It employed several thousand people in Fairport and the surrounding area.

Joe Dolce's grandfather retired from the company, which he said provided a good living for families. It was just down the road from his childhood home.

> *I used to spend hours as a kid climbing the huge story-high mounds of gravel, chemicals, and whatever else was piled around it. And the large yellow and green man-made lake we called "Soup Pond." I worked nights there one summer. Never forget the almost unbearable smell of chemicals flowing on the conveyer belt. No masks in those days.*

Kristi Lockwood grew up in Painesville and says her grandfather George Saari, the first sibling in his family born in America after the Saaris came from Finland in the early 1900s, worked there from 1928 to 1962. Saari, who lived in Painesville all his life, worked in the millroom. Kristi discovered photos in her grandparents' album of him in front of Fairport Oil, which she thinks was connected to the plant, where he may have worked first.

Her grandfather's six-inch-thick scrapbook is filled with scores for the Diamond Alkali bowling and baseball teams he was on. A late 1930s clipping with the headline "Diamond Softball Loop Launches 9th Season" says, "Play opened in the Diamond Alkali softball league Tuesday night when Millroom and Caustic tens dropped opponents. The Millroom whipped the Office team, 9–4, and the Caustic ten dropped the Boiler Shop, 2–1."

Fourteen teams from different departments played on a field on the bank of the lake, west of the plant's main office, with games starting at six thirty in the evening. Other games were played at Willoughbeach Park in what is today Willowick. A 1930 headline reads: "Saari Wins in Sun-Tan Event."

George Saari, of Painesville, in front of the Fairport Oil Co. in 1927. *Photo courtesy of Kristi Lockwood, from the personal collection of George and Garnet Saari.*

Construction of the Diamond Alkali Plant. *Courtesy of Dennis Lawrence, from the personal collection of his father, Edward S. Lawrence Jr.*

George won the men's weekly miniature golf course tournament with a score of forty-six.

Dennis Lawrence's father, Edward S. Lawrence Jr., born in Perry in 1905, started working at Diamond Alkali in 1933. He worked as a carpenter during the construction of part of the plant and in the chromate plant, which later caused lung cancer for him and many others. He retired in 1967 as area superintendent in charge of shipping. Although it wasn't recognized at the time, the caustic chemicals created an unsafe workplace, causing cancer and other medical problems for employees years later.

In 1967, the company merged with Shamrock Oil and Gas Company to become the Diamond Shamrock Corp. During peak years, it employed five thousand people and had its own fleet of buses to transport workers from Painesville. By the time the Diamond, as it was known by locals, closed in 1976, it had decreased to one thousand employees.

Here Is Ohio's Lake County says the company's more than six decades of operation created an environmental disaster. When the 1,100-acre site, on the border of Painesville and Fairport Harbor, was investigated in the '90s, environmental officials discovered 750,000 tons of chromate materials, three waste lakes and other toxic contaminants, as well as runoff into the Grand River and Lake Erie.

The Ohio Environmental Protection Agency and the companies that existed on the site brokered a multimillion-dollar deal to clean up the area, which has become the largest brownfield recovery project in the state, known as the Hemisphere Project or Lakeview Bluffs.

RUMRUNNING

From 1920 to 1933, during Prohibition, the sale, manufacture and transportation of alcoholic beverages was illegal. However, rumrunning, the act of illegally transporting alcohol over a body of water, was still big business.

The Atlantic and Gulf of Mexico were notorious rumrunning regions, but cities along the Great Lakes were also hot spots to smuggle in booze (particularly whiskey, brandy and beer). There were even reports of airplanes transporting alcohol illegally over the lakes.

Rumrunning tales abound in Lake County; however, it can be difficult to differentiate between fact and legend. Brian Dickey, who lived in Mentor for years, recalls tales of rumrunning passed down through the generations. "My grandfather Warren Dickey would tell stories about hearing the rumrunners that used to come ashore on Lake Erie at the end of Chestnut Street in Mentor-on-the-Lake to deliver liquor from Canada during Prohibition," said Dickey.

The Mentor Marsh Inn was located on Lakeshore Boulevard where the Amvets Post currently is, next door to the Breakwall Tavern. "His [Warren Dickey's] in-laws (Robert and Nellie Babcock) owned the inn, and he and my grandmother Irene lived in a house behind it in the early 1930s."

Around that time, Warren's father, Lawrence Dickey, was elected as one of three Lake County commissioners, and he got Warren a job as park manager at Mentor Beach Park, which was about one-quarter mile west of the inn. "While living at the park manager's house, my grandfather would hear motors of the rumrunner boats pull up to the docks in the middle of the night to unload their liquor for the inn."

Dickey's family roots run deep in county history. His relative Colonel Warren Corning led a wagon train from New Hampshire to Mentor in 1819. "His traveling companions bestowed him the title of colonel for his efficient leadership of the wagon train. Two of Warren Corning's daughters, Rachel and Harriet, married two Dickey brothers, George and James." George and Rachel were Dickey's great-great-great-great grandparents, and they had

Left: Robert Babcock, who ran the Mentor Marsh Inn until he passed away in 1940; his wife, Nellie, continued running it until the mid-1950s, when she sold it. *Courtesy of Brian Dickey.*

Below: Nellie Babcock (*left*), who ran the Mentor Marsh for more than a decade, and her daughter Irene (*right*). Believed to be at the little dock at the end of Chestnut Street behind the Mentor Marsh Inn. *Courtesy of Brian Dickey.*

farms connected by Dickey Road. Part of Dickey Road was eventually sold to James Garfield, and Dickey Road was renamed Garfield Road.

Another great-great-great-great grandfather was Joseph Rider, who opened Rider's Inn in 1812. "It was purportedly a safe haven for runaway slaves traveling along the Underground Railroad before the Civil War," said Dickey. "I never heard any firsthand stories about this from my grandfather, however. The inn was sold to George Randall in 1902, and he opened a speakeasy at the inn during Prohibition."

Despite the laws against it, alcohol was also available by land and made its way to speakeasys and private parties. Charles Otis, a wealthy industrialist from Cleveland, was known to entertain famous people like actors Will Rogers and Ethel Barrymore at his Waite Hill estate, Pine Tree Farm. He continued to host parties during Prohibition. According to Otis's 1951 autobiography, *Here I Am*, he and his friend Jack Sherwin, a businessman and Waite Hill property owner, purchased $30,000 in cases of Old Crow Bourbon and several hundred cases of the best brands of scotch from the William Edwards Company, which was a pioneer manufacturer and wholesaler of food products in Cleveland.

"Jack Sherwin was very fond of what he called 'Orange Blossoms' which were gin and orange juice," explained Otis. So they bought the ingredients, including gin (nine dollars a case), champagne (thirty dollars a case) and vermouth (one dollar a case.) They had quite a collection, which they stored in a cellar under Sherwin's house on Overlook Road. Otis writes,

> He obtained some vault doors from the First National Bank, and we were set. When we wished to take stimulants to the farm, we would stop there, put a case or two in our cars, and take them out to Waite Hill. At one time this accumulation of liquor, had we been bootleggers, could have been disposed of in the neighborhood of $300,000. Not for us; it was more pleasure to see our little friends come out and invigorate themselves!

In his book, Otis recalls hosting the Detroit polo team at his farm on a Sunday and putting up a sign on his house saying, "Anyone who voted dry cannot get a drink here."

> I recall one of the most intimate friends, a great industrialist, was so shocked at the sign he said, "Tot [as he was known by friends], you don't mean that." And I said, "I mean it but you know I couldn't see you faint away on the porch." So, we went on purveying these great stimulants

for years. Jack and I figured that we had purchased enough real old liquor to last us through our lives, but there seemed to be a sign in the air that a person could get a real drink at Sherwin's or Otis', and inside of nine years we were depleted!

Fishing

"Lake Erie was an incredibly abundant source of food, producing as much fish as all the other Great Lakes combined," according to *Here Is Ohio's Lake County*. "Commercial fishing fleets had easy access to the lake through protected harbors on the Chagrin and Grand Rivers."

Grandon, incorporated in 1836, located at the mouth of the Grand River, was a thriving port and village. (Its name changed to Fairport, with "Harbor" added later.)

Grand River was a natural location to discharge the day's catch and for processing and storage facilities. *History of Mentor Headlands and Vicinity* says that in 1892, the oldest fishing industries were Hough and Grows. "Searles had the first grocery store, which was also a general store and post office. Dances were held in the Harrison block and were called Fisherman's Balls. Fawn Ely played the fiddle; Bob Whitney the dulcimer, which he made himself."

Evan's Lunchroom (now Brennan's Fish House) was a famous saloon, quenching fishermen's thirst for just five cents per bucket of beer.

The population in Grand River in 1857 was more than two thousand, but since the 1950s, it has remained around four hundred.

In 1869, Charles Ruggles, who introduced net fishing in Fairport, caught 1,500 sturgeons in his first season. There wasn't a market for sturgeon because locals weren't familiar with eating it, so Ruggels sold them to Storrs and Harrison Nursery for one dollar a wagonload to use as fertilizer. In 1915, a sturgeon was caught that was fifty-eight inches long and fifty-seven pounds.

Before 1900, Lake County fishermen used nets hung from stakes driven into the bottom of the lake spaced apart in a line to create a fish trap or drag seines, which were fishing nets hung vertically in the water with a weight on the bottom and a float attached to the top.

In the early 1900s, fishing was good; the catch at Grand River ranged between one to two million pounds and included lake herring, blue pike, carp, yellow perch, sauger, lake whitefish, walleye and sturgeon.

Here Is Ohio's Lake County reads: "Good fishing lasted for over 40 years.

Grand River Fish Company workers circa 1920s. *Courtesy of Bill Smith.*

About a mile of navigable river frontage in the Village of Grand River was owned by fishing companies; The Grow Brothers, The Kishman Fish Company, Buckeye Fisheries, and the Dominish Brothers."

Gradually, catches declined, and by the late 1960s, there was no commercial fishing left at Grand River.

MARTIN BROTHERS

Four Martin brothers, from Madison, were known for their maritime business ventures in the mid-twentieth century. Bob and Ralph operated Martin Brothers Marina, originally an old icehouse for Kishman Fish Company, in Grand River, where Pickle Bill's restaurant now stands. Bob's sons Timothy and Terry Martin say it was the first marina in the area with a full-service restaurant, called Charlie's Boat Drive-In, allowing boaters to drive up their boat and get food, like barbeque chicken, brought out to them and first with a lift to remove boats from the water and move them inside for repairs or storage. At one point, the marina was destroyed by a fire.

The Martin brothers also opened a boat and supply store on Mentor Avenue, next to Saint Mary's Catholic Church, in 1962.

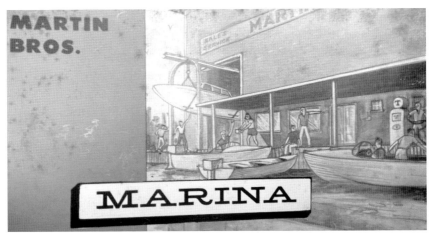

Top: Cover of a Martin Bros. Marina promotional brochure. *Courtesy of Timothy Martin.*

Bottom: Photo of the four Martin brothers in a Martin Bros. Marina brochure. *Left to right*: Ralph, Chuck, Bob and Stan. *Courtesy of Timothy Martin.*

Stan and Chuck operated a boat-building business at Mentor Harbor Yacht Club. They built the forty-three-foot *Water Witch* for Harold F. Seymor of Cleveland, which won the Falcon Cup in 1950 (raced between Cleveland Yachting Club and Mentor Harbor Yachting Club since 1938).

Each year, Falcon Cup participants are reminded: "Don't forget to catch your bag of ice in the channel after the race." This comes from a legend

by land or by sea . . .

the many services of Martin Bros. Marina are easily available to YOU! Complete, courteous water-side service for boat, motor or hungry skipper and crew are yours for the asking. Own a boat? Fine — take advantage of 500 feet of deep-water dock at Martin Bros. . . . the boat ramp . . . famous Texaco marine products . . . motor service (mechanic always on duty) . . . winter storage inside. If you don't own one—RENT ONE! Everything you need—from a run-a-bout to a cruiser, complete with water skis, food and cold drinks can be rented by the hour, day or month. Call ahead and Martin Bros. will have your pleasure craft gassed, provisioned and ready to go!

Featuring:

Charlie's Boat Drive-in with **Plump** and **Pampered** Barbecue Chicken — piping hot and ready to go — along with other delectable treats.
Tel.: EL. 2-2949

Call "The Marina" on your ship-to-shore and your food and drink orders will be ready and waiting when you arrive.

MARTIN BROS.

"Call the 'Marina' on your ship-to-shore, and your food and drink orders will be ready and waiting when you arrive." *Courtesy of Timothy Martin.*

that the originators of the Falcon Cup were out of ice for their drinks by the end of the race (there were no refrigerators or boat coolers back then) and demanded more ice on their way in.

ICE HARVESTING

When Lake Erie froze in the late nineteenth/early twentieth centuries, ice skating and ice boating, sailing craft supported on metal runners to travel over ice, were very popular in Fairport Harbor. Ice also provided a source of survival. It was harvested by scoring and cutting sections by saw. The ice, stored in wooden icehouses filled with sawdust along the river, was used to preserve fish and food sent to suppliers. Most homes also had iceboxes, which held up to fifty pounds of ice. Ice was also harvested in other spots along the lake and rivers, like the Chagrin River.

Many remember their houses shaking in Eastlake and Willoughby and a rumbling sound as far as Kirtland as explosives were set off in the Chagrin

River in Eastlake to break up the ice and prevent flooding. For several decades, through the 1970s, the Dynamite Devils were a hardy group of men risking their lives by using gasoline drills to cut holes in the ice, placing charges through the holes and setting off the dynamite electronically, forcing the broken ice to burst skyward. They blasted ice beginning at the mouth of the Chagrin and working south toward Lakeshore Boulevard, with some of the most dangerous bends, where ice jammed, just to the north.

On January 20, 1959, heavy rain fell on six inches of snow, causing damaging flooding in the Chagrin Valley, aggravated by ice jamming at the mouth of the river. Weather reports predicted warm temperatures and rain, known to cause trouble along the river, especially when it was covered with ice.

"The ice is one foot thick at the Lake Shore Blvd. bridge, but the water is running freely underneath the ice," said service director John W. Howells in a January 1969 *Cleveland Press* article. "The problem is we have had a lot of snow and a hard freeze, as far up as Gates Mills and Chagrin Falls, and we will get it all when this stuff melts."

Monitoring crews reported ice movements and water levels hourly from Chagrin Falls, Gates Mills, Willoughby Hills and Willoughby. "When we

"Dynamite Devils" place dynamite, preparing to blast an ice jam in the Chagrin River, December 20, 1937. *Courtesy of Eastlake Historical Society.*

Man trying to keep ice chunks away from his home after ice on the Chagrin River was broken up by dynamite, 1942. *Courtesy of Eastlake Historical Society.*

get a report that ice has broken loose in Chagrin Falls, we know that in two hours it will be in Eastlake and we have to get ready to blast if the ice jams," Howells explained.

On December 27 the same year, Eastlake was forced to evacuate forty families to temporary aid stations as the river flooded the lowlands south of Lakeshore Boulevard and rose rapidly from its normal depth of four to ten feet.

Several public works projects managed the portions of the river with the most severe flooding, and the dyno devils are no longer needed.

GIANT MYSTERY WAVES

Imagine you're gazing at the calm water on Lake Erie, when suddenly a giant mystery wave washes toward you. It's happened several times over the years, in 1882, 1942 and 1952. The 1882 wave was said to be more than eight feet tall and came ashore at 6:20 a.m., carrying huge logs and debris hundreds of feet inland.

Seven people drowned in the 1942 wave, which was reported to be up to fifteen feet high, stretching from Bay Village to Geneva. About ten minutes before the wave hit, there were reports of distant thunder offshore and a heavy cloud over the lake, but there were no reports of strong winds or an earthquake. It's believed that violent thunderstorm winds several miles offshore of Cleveland created a large wave that moved inland.

Again in 1952, a surge of water and up to twenty-foot-high waves hit the coast from Euclid to Fairport. According to an article in the *Plain Dealer*, the following day, windows were smashed and framework ripped off cottages in Eastlake. The most seriously damaged properties were on Galalina, Matoma and Wanaka Streets.

Alex Melbourne, who owned an eight-room "year-round house," said it was the worst wave he had seen in his thirty-two years of residence. "For one thing, the wall of water was higher. Also, this year there are only 10 to 15 feet of beach whereas, in former years, there have been 200 feet." He said his brother was sleeping on a cot on the back porch when the wave swept past him through the home and washed away a side porch.

According to a June 30, 1952 article in the *News-Herald*, "Mrs. William J. Sasso, of Parkway Dr., Eastlake, said the wave was a sight she 'wouldn't have missed for anything.'" She watched it from her home's upstairs window, about twenty feet from the lake. "Just before it hit, I saw the high wall of water and it was the most beautiful shade of emerald I've ever seen. It rolled in like a solid wall and made a soothing, swishing sound." Their home wasn't damaged, but their yard was "terribly cluttered."

In Willowick, Eddie DeMore was at the beach with a friend, standing with their backs to the lake, cooking hot dogs. "The next thing they knew they were swamped with water. They lost their shoes and portable radio."

Down the shore at Mentor Harbor Yacht Club, a seventy-five-foot section of retainer wall was washed away, although the well-secured boats were not damaged.

Shipwrecks

Marshall F. Butters

High winds and treacherous weather can wreak havoc on the waters of Lake Erie very quickly due to its shallow depth. This sudden change has caught many mariners off guard.

In 1916, the ten survivors of the foundered steamer *Marshall F. Butters* came into Fairport aboard two other steamers. The Massillon *Evening Independent* reported that the *Butters,* a wooden craft carrying a cargo of lumber to Cleveland, was helplessly swept into heavy seas for hours before most of the crew abandoned it on lifeboats. The three men left aboard jumped over the side as the steamer plunged below and waited thirty minutes before the crew of another steamer came to rescue them.

Queen of the West

In the early morning hours of August 20, 1903, the *Queen of the West* departed Cleveland loaded with 1,500 tons of iron ore. It was built in Bay City, Michigan, in 1881; was 215 feet long, with a wooden hull and a single steam-powered propeller; and was headed to Erie, Pennsylvania, carrying fifteen people when it sprung a serious leak and began filling with water around four in the morning.

The pumps couldn't keep up as water poured in, so Captain Massey ordered the flag set to half-mast to signal distress. Lifeboats were launched, but high

Queen of the West. Courtesy of the Historical Collections of the Great Lakes, Bowling Green State University.

winds and strong waves capsized them. The steamer *Codorus* was luckily headed westward and saw the distressed ship, and all fifteen people aboard were saved.

According to the Fairport Harbor Historical Society, the lookout at USLSS Station Fairport saw the distress signal at five o'clock in the morning and launched their lifeboat and harbor tug, *Kitty Downs*, into the lake. Massey and two mates boarded the *Kitty Downs* and were taken to the Station Fairport, while everyone else stayed on the *Corodus* and were brought to Cleveland.

Later that morning, the harbor tug *James Byers* took Massey and the two mates back to the sinking ship to recover clothes and valuables. A short while later, according to the USLSS Station Fairport logbook, the *Queen of the West* sank in twelve fathoms of water, eight miles northwest of Fairport.

In 1975, several dives were made to the wreck, and artifacts, including the ship's whistle, were recently donated to the Fairport Harbor Historical Society.

Edmund Fitzgerald

It was supposed to be Edward "Eddie" Bindon's last trip as an assistant engineer before retiring. The army veteran and Fairport resident planned to spend more time with his ailing mother and wife, Helen, of twenty-five years, after his final launch aboard the *Edmund Fitzgerald*.

Unfortunately, this trip truly was the last for him—and for everyone else on board.

One of the most infamous modern-day Great Lakes shipwrecks happened in Lake Superior on November 10, 1975, during a gale of near-hurricane-force winds and blinding snow squalls. The $8.4 million vessel was the largest ever built on the Great Lakes when it launched from Michigan in 1958, loaded with ore and bound for Cleveland—and disappeared from radar and sank in a matter of ten minutes. All twenty-nine crew members died.

Bindon's niece, Debbie Sposit, remembers him as a large man with an even larger presence. "When Eddie walked into the room, you knew it." Sposit says she was fortunate enough to sail with him twice: once on a freighter called the *Armco* and then on the *Fitzgerald* (both ships were in the Oglebay Norton fleet).

"I sailed on the Fitzgerald in August of 1975. I was twelve," remembered Sposit. "Eddie told me that this would be the last trip I would be able to make with him. The next year, I would be a teenager, and there were many young men working the boats in the summer....In retrospect, I would have probably had the summer of my life had that been able to happen."

Above: Edward "Eddie" and Helen Bindon. *Courtesy of Deb Sposit.*

Right: Deb Sposit aboard the *Edmund Fitzgerald. Courtesy of Deb Sposit.*

American Great Lakes freighter the SS *Edmund Fitzgerald. Courtesy of the Historical Collections of the Great Lakes, Bowling Green State University.*

Sposit said they traveled to Detroit to board the *Fitz* and remembers being hoisted up in a basket by the crew, which she said was a little scary. To a young girl, the ship was enormous. "Taconite or iron ore is red. Most of the time, I was covered in this red dust. During the day, I could freely wander around the boat, and in the evening, we'd have dinner and play cards. These were very warm memories."

Sposit remembers many of the crew members, including Captain McSorley, who let her sit in the pilot house while passing through the Soo Locks. "The *Fitz* being such a large ship would always draw a crowd. Captain McSorley would lay on the horn and watch the crowd jump."

Sposit said the day the ship sank, she was in school and unaware. Her father picked her up at lunch and told her what happened on the way to her aunt's house, where her family was awaiting news. "This was before the internet or twenty-four-hour news stations, so we relied on any news out of radio stations out of Detroit or official phone calls from Oglebay Norton. It was several days before we got word that they were calling off the search and there were no survivors. Devastating for sure."

Sposit said that without a body, burial was even more difficult, and she remembers traveling to the Maritime Sailors Cathedral for a service. "They did a roll call and rang the bell for each crew member," she said. "Each family placed a wreath in the water." Bindon's family later held a memorial for him at St. Anthony's in Fairport, and her aunt had a headstone made with his name on it.

According to Bindon's niece Fran Gabor, in a *Detroit News* article, days after her uncle died, her aunt Helen (Eddie's wife) received an unexpected delivery. While in Duluth, Minnesota, Eddie had bought his wife a two-carat diamond ring as a surprise twenty-fifth wedding anniversary gift and gave it to a friend to keep safe. "For some reason, he didn't want to take it aboard the ship," said Gabor. "He just had an ominous feeling—at least that's how it seems. My aunt never re-married and she wore that ring for the rest of her life." Helen died in 1981, and many believe she died of a broken heart.

The two-hundred-pound bell from the *Fitzgerald*, recovered from the site in 1995, is on display in the Great Lakes Shipwreck Museum on Whitefish Point, Michigan. In its place, divers left a replica bell inscribed with the names of the lost crew, including Eddie's, to serve as a permanent grave marker.

Lost Graves of the *G.P. Griffith*

In the predawn hours of June 17, 1850, off the coast of present-day Willowick, a fire blazed out on the water. Residents who were up early in this farming community saw flames shooting up, illuminating the still-dark morning sky.

The *G.P. Griffith* steamboat, traveling from Buffalo, New York, to Toledo, carrying about 326 passengers (including many European immigrants), was engulfed in flames. There are several theories as to what started the fire: water tanks around the ship's pipes were dry; a "fire-resistant" oil applied to the ship turned out to be very flammable; paint, stored too close to the firebox, overheated and burst into flames. There was even a theory that the captain had been drunk and/or racing another ship.

No matter the cause, the results were catastrophic. Although the ship was only one-half mile away from shore, it became stuck on a sandbar while heading inland. People began jumping into the lake, but most didn't know how to swim and drowned in only nine feet of water.

Hundreds of bodies were recovered, and most were buried in mass graves; however, their location has remained a mystery for nearly two centuries. Some accounts say they were buried on the sand, but newspaper articles from the time say they were buried on a bluff, far back from the water. Those

Drawing of the *G.P. Griffith* engulfed in flames. *Courtesy of Willoughby Historical Society.*

who lived on the lake were farmers and fishermen, familiar with the effects of nature, so it's likely they had the foresight to bury the bodies away from the edge.

A July 2, 1981 newspaper clipping found in the City of Willowick archives, reflecting on the long-ago event, backs up that idea:

> *A team of oxen was yoked to a plow to dig more trenches for the great graves, thirty feet long, six feet wide, and eight feet deep near the knoll of the bank of the lake a little to the East. Men and women were laid in rows, children were packed to fill the spaces. Bodies were carried up to the trenches for days....Many were buried on the bank of the lake on the farm owned by Ransom Kennedy.*

The November 25, 1898 *Willoughby Independent* says Captain Kennedy, owner of the schooner *Saginaw*, lived on the lakeshore and was one of the first to arrive at the scene. An 1857 map shows Kennedy's farm stretching from approximately the western edge of Lakefront Lodge to the western edge of the Larimar housing development across from Shoregate Shopping Center and a good distance south.

Levi Mosher owned lakefront property bordering Kennedy's to the northwest, which Cindy Channell-Kurzinger (descendant of Levi's brother John) discovered in an 1850 tax assessment. (Kennedy later bought this land from Levi.)

Many think the *Griffith* sank close to Lakefront Lodge, perhaps because this is the site of a historical marker. However, numerous records point to

61

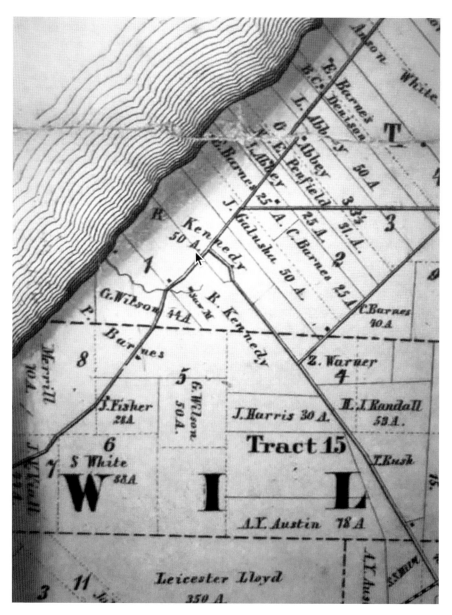

An 1857 map of Willoughby, present-day Willowick, showing property of Ransom Kennedy along the lakeshore. *Courtesy of Lakecountyohio.gov.*

the *Griffith* sinking farther to the west, along a stretch of coastline between Cresthaven and East 305th Street (now covered with homes), Larimar (excavators say nothing was uncovered while clearing the land), and a private neighborhood beach club, Willo Beach Park (the former site of Willoughbeach Amusement Park), that spans the grounds and contains an original pavilion and cement platform that, according to maps, appears to be where the park's main pavilion once stood.

An account from the City of Willowick archives reads,

> *We buried 87 in one grave. There have been a good many things said about the grave being opened and robbed, but Henry M. Mosher [son of Levi] says the statement is untrue. The grave was on his father's farm. I always thought that when we buried those bodies, we buried a lot of money in the petticoats of the women.*

According to maps from the time, Levi's property line and the creek alongside it, the burial ground would have been near the mouth of the creek, between Willo Beach Park and the western edge of Larimar. Part of the land, particularly on the eastern end, has eroded since then, but there were never reports of mass amounts of bodies washing into the lake in the years following the disaster.

In fact, that may not be where the bodies remained, because a June 20, 1850 *Plain Dealer* article says a Cleveland committee planned to exhume ninety-four bodies from one grave to bring to the city for individual interment and sent two scows to return with the bodies that afternoon. Coffins were prepared, and funeral ceremonies were planned to take place at Public Square. Then, for unknown reasons, plans changed, and the committee decided to purchase and enclose one half acre of land on the bank of the lake opposite the wreck, exhume the bodies, "make memorandums as to personal identity" and number and bury each body separately. "This will give all the information possible to surviving friends." However, after attempting to remove several bodies on a hot June day, they changed their minds and decided to dig two long trenches "into which the bodies will be placed at moderate distances apart and at the head of each one elevated above the ground will appear either on wood or stone the name as such as are known and the numbers of all. Those numbers and names will also be kept in a book and opposite each, such memorandum as may have been taken of the person." It seems the bodies were reinterred; however, the grave markers were never found.

Several months later, Levi and his wife, Silvia, were said to have sold the mass grave on their property to the City of Cleveland for five dollars to be preserved as a cemetery. Perhaps this is the site of the reinterment? According to the Lake County Genealogical Society, the document, signed on September 5, 1850, describes the site as one quarter acre of land in the northwest corner of the tract, with the western edge of the land a small gully. The document stated that the city could go through the Levis' land to reach the site if their crops weren't injured in the process. "Said piece of land to be used as a burying ground, and for no other purposes, but subject to all legal highways."

Kennedy and Mosher's land was later sold to farmer George Wilson for eighty-five dollars an acre and in 1893 to the Shaker Vineyard Company, which sold it to the Cleveland, Painesville and Eastern syndicate to build Willoughbeach Park and to Willowick Country Club.

Six decades after the tragedy, a news clipping in Willowick City Hall describes a disturbing scene at Willoughbeach Amusement Park.

> *On the crumbling edge of a bluff overlooking the bathing beach at Willoughbeach, and within a few feet of the dance hall, those who go to that pleasure resort have lately been attracted by the remains of a wooden box which juts out from the top of the cliff, three feet below its brow.*

The box, although "crumbling into dust," was a coffin made of black walnut and believed to contain a victim of the shipwreck.

> *Two elongated bones, presumably shin bones, have been taken from the box, according to General Manager Charles F. Fisher, of the amusement park, whether there are any more bones remains to be determined, because cave-ins of ground have filled what was exposed to the action of the wind toward the lake, and Fisher says he'll not have the place disturbed.*

At the time of the disaster, many of the bodies were buried in black walnut coffins one half mile back from the beach and, when they ran out of wood, in trenches.

"An Anonymous Tale of Willobeach Park by Alphy Deeh" gives Deeh's accounts of working at the park in the early 1920s, inspecting and cleaning the merry-go-round. "My job was made up of two parts—one part the public saw every day, and one part the public never saw." Deeh says the cliff, where the victims were buried, had partially eroded.

Willoughbeach Amusement Park, in present-day Willowick. *Courtesy of City of Willowick.*

So, the secret part of my job was to go down on the beach every morning before the park opened and inspect the cliff for any projecting bones. These I would remove and dispose of. I found several arm and leg bones, and some ribs. I also found a pelvis and a skull, which I lost in a card game.

For years, the area was the site of merrymaking as people enjoyed the rides, ate at the picnic tables and gazed out at the lake; all the while, most didn't know its connection to a tragic past. However, like Alphy, some visitors did make discoveries.

A newspaper clipping states:

It is said that long after the tragedy, folks would go to the beach for a summer day outing and often a picnic as well, and would see a hand, a leg or part of an arm sticking out of the lake bank. They complained to authorities that this goulish [sic] site was ruining their outings and insisted that more dirt be added to the graved bank. This was done repeatedly until at last the corpses stayed buried.

Based on old photos, postcards and foundational remnants, the main pavilion, rides and baseball fields of Willoughbeach were all west of the creek, stretching across part of Cresthaven and possibly Sylvan and Bruce, along with some of the western Larimar homes. The bathing beaches were to the east, connected by several bridges that crossed the creek. Willowick Country Club existed simultaneously, during the park's later years, with the clubhouse located on the eastern side of the creek at Kennedy's former home.

Because hundreds of people were buried, it's possible there was a mass grave, as documented by Levi on one side of the creek, and perhaps another on the other side.

Channell-Kurzinger discovered that twenty-four victims of the *Griffith* appear to have been buried in Erie Street Cemetery in Cleveland, in two plots of twelve, perhaps funded by the cemetery, the city or money found on the bodies.

One of the survivors, Henry Priday (sometimes spelled Pridey) was traveling on the *Griffith* with his extended family. According to a letter written by Priday that Channell-Kurzinger shared with me, Priday was the only one to survive, and he was said to have stayed at the wreckage for ten days, searching for his family. Levi saw how distraught he was and offered to bury his family in the Mosher family cemetery for free. The cemetery was located across from the Old Mosher Farmhouse at Ridge Road and 300th Street, on the south side (where Lake Metroparks Pete's Pond Preserve is today). Buried there were his daughter, Kate, and his wife, Elizabeth, perhaps along with several other relatives and victims of the *Griffith*.

Levi's eight-year-old nephew, George, came home to the farmhouse the day after the wreck and made a chilling discovery, according to Eleanor Rolf's book, *Willoughby Schools, the First 100 Years.* "He noticed wagon tracks in the drive leading to the barn—tracks that had been freshly made." Thinking visitors had arrived, he went into the barn to investigate and discovered a cover over the wagon. "He lifted the cover and peeked in. Horrors, there lay a wagon load of human bodies; the faces and hair were bedraggled with lake sand and the clothing was water soaked. Frightened almost out of his boots he ran breathlessly to his mother."

She explained it was the bodies of Mr. Priday's family, who would be buried in the Mosher cemetery.

Roger Tetzlaff, current owner of the Old Mosher Farmhouse, discovered an 1850 cemetery map showing that Levi deeded the small section of land to the mayor of Cleveland for preservation as an official cemetery. The document has a hand-drawn map that includes markers for the cemetery plot and Mosher and Ridge Roads. I contacted the deed department for the city of Cleveland to see if the deed was ever transferred again but have yet to hear back.

The bodies of the Mosher family are believed to have been reinterred in 1926, but there is no record for Henry's family. The cemetery was later dismantled, and its stones were said to be buried under people's patios and used in paving around 300th Street.

THE UNDERGROUND RAILROAD

Due to its location along the lake, the county became an outlet for slaves escaping to freedom in Canada through the Underground Railroad (a network of people, and locations, who hid slaves and helped them along the route).

According to historian Lee Silvi, Fairport Harbor was the terminus on the thirteen-mile Liberty Line, which extended from Chardon to Concord to Painesville and then on to Fairport. Once in Fairport, several locations were involved, including the former Eagle Tavern, located down the hill from the lighthouse; the basement of the lighthouse keeper's dwelling, with the assistance of abolitionist lighthouse keepers; a warehouse owned by Phineas Root, one of nearly a dozen warehouses between the lighthouse and the river; houses at 129 Eagle Street (still there) and 219 Eagle Street (demolished); and the Fairmount on Third Street. According to Silvi, there are stories of some slaves even hiding on the hillside.

Legend has it that some of the vessel captains hung out at the Eagle Tavern, and if one was known to be an abolitionist, the tavern keeper and/ or lighthouse keeper would arrange to help the slaves escape to the vessel.

It's claimed that the lighthouse keepers alone helped at least one hundred slaves escape to freedom, and about 40 percent of the thirty to forty thousand slaves using the Underground Railroad to escape did so through Ohio. Several Underground Railroad routes are believed to have converged in Concord, according to *Here Is Ohio's Lake County*. One came from Akron, Hudson and Chagrin Falls and another from Ravenna.

Up to one hundred slaves are said to have once gathered in Seth Marshall's barn at the corner of Walnut and Bank Streets on Painesville's riverbank. "They were sent downstream to Fairport or whisked across the river to C.C. Jennings' on Casement Avenue or Uri Seeley's on Riverside Drive, to be out of the way of inquiring agents," reads *Here Is Ohio's Lake County*.

Eber D. Howe was an abolitionist who was also the founder of the *Painesville Telegraph*. He was one of the early editors in the county to take a firm stance on local news and issues, including slavery and Mormonism.

Cynthia and Hawley Drake.
Courtesy of Susan Clark.

According to *Here Is Ohio's Lake County*, he's also credited with introducing a new word, stemming from a local incident.

> *A group of counterfeiters were discovered in Painesville and their machine was "a great wonderment for some time among the crowd that had collected around....Many remarks and suggestions were made as to the name it bore or the one which should be given it....Finally, someone called it a "Bogus." The word "bogus" appeared twice in the Telegraph in 1827 as a description for the fraudulent operations of counterfeiting, and it has remained in our vocabulary with much of its original meaning.*

Around 1836, Howe moved from Mentor Avenue to what is now Lake Metroparks Big Creek at Liberty Hollow, in Concord Township, which has been known by several names, including Drake Hollow and Howe Hollow, through which a creek runs from Chardon to the Grand River near Painesville.

While there, Howe was an active agent for the Underground Railroad—believed to have helped hundreds of enslaved people escape along Fay

Road—while also managing an iron furnace, sawmill and woolen mill from the site. When Howe moved out in 1856, Hawley Drake moved in, according to his descendant Susan Clark. Drake married Cynthia Wheeler of Madison, and they had three children. They took over operations of the woolen mill from Howe until it was destroyed by a fire in 1865. (It was later repaired by Hawley's brother, Addison, and began operating again in 1870, lasting another five years).

According to Clark, Hawley became a farmer, serving as president of the Lake County Agricultural Society and a correspondent for the *Painesville Telegraph*. The family lived happily for many years in what became known as Drake's Hollow.

By 1838, the Reserve had a more definite antislavery character than any other territory of a similar size in the United States.

In 1861, the U.S. ship *Star of the West* was fired on in Charleston Harbor while bringing supplies to besieged Fort Sumter. Lake County leaders reacted by calling a mass meeting to consider "the perilous state of the Union." Enthusiasm and public sentiment were so strong that men unable to attend had to publicly explain the reason for their absence.

"In Painesville's Courthouse, those at the meeting agreed to do all possible 'to preserve the present form of government' and 'that prompt vigorous action alone could preserve the Union.' Lake Countians indicated that they would rather lose their government than be found guilty of ignoring their obligations to it," reads *Here Is Ohio's Lake County*.

Soon after their meeting, Abraham Lincoln himself stopped at the Painesville train station on his way to Washington for his inauguration, speaking to a crowd of more than four hundred. The local press commented on his remarks and observed, "This man is not nearly as odd in appearance as previous reports had indicated."

Chapter 4

TRAINS AND TRANSPORTATION

I loved to hear that trolley
That hummed so merrily,
The whistle shrill, I hear it still
On the cars of the CP&E.
—Author unknown

The first lines of transportation into the Western Reserve, and what would become Lake County, were stagecoaches. By 1816, the first stagecoach line from Cleveland to Buffalo was established, and although it improved travel, it was tedious and unpredictable.

According to *Here Is Ohio's Lake County*, an old issue of the *Painesville Republican* tells the story of a runaway stagecoach. The driver, Frank Bryant, was on his way to Cleveland with a mother and daughter as passengers. "At the Rider Tavern a stop was made while Bryant went inside to exchange greetings with the landlord and get a little something to take the 'wire edge off his whistle.' The horses became frightened and started to run, taking with them the coach and passengers."

When Bryant realized his rig was gone, he ran to the barn, saddled a horse and headed west. Although he was in sight of the coach several times, he couldn't catch up until reaching Willoughby.

At the doorway of the Willoughby Tavern the coach horses stopped as neatly as though the driver had been in the box, and Bryant was just in time to jump off his horse and open the coach door for his passengers. When the lady alighted Bryant expected she would be either frightened or mad, but instead she smiled and shook his hand, remarking, "You are the first real driver we've had since we left Buffalo."

Travel by steamship along Lake Erie could also be hazardous, as storms quickly churned up the waters, and it was halted in the winter months when the lake froze. Local merchants and residents needed dependable connections to eastern and western markets.

A group of local citizens saw the rapid growth of the railroad in Cleveland as it became the Lake Terminal, or northern outlet, for the Ohio Canal so they obtained a charter in 1835 for the Painesville & Fairport Railroad. Master builder Jonathan Goldsmith agreed to oversee the construction of the tracks—oak rails with thin strips of iron to cover them—and two years later, they were opened from Fairport Harbor to Painesville. This was the second railroad operating in Ohio, but it opened during a severe depression, and money to build ran out. By 1841, flooding from a spring thaw carried away the bridge near Skinner's Landing, but the company didn't have funds to rebuild, so the tracks became overgrown with weeds.

"Northeast Ohio was destined to become a major transportation corridor in the 1850s; it was directly in the path of the railroads stretching westward from eastern markets to Chicago," according to Mark J. Camp's *Railroad Depots of Northeast Ohio*. "Some of Ohio's earliest railroads were projected to connect Lake Erie with the Ohio River and points south."

Since Cleveland was a major lake and canal port, it was an ideal hub to connect larger cities across the Midwest with smaller cities in northeast Ohio.

THE INTERURBANS

Below the concrete of many Lake County streets lie the remnants of an earlier time: the tracks of the interurban railways.

The Cleveland, Painesville, & Eastern (CP&E) was an electric rail line running from Public Square in downtown Cleveland to Painesville and, eventually, to Ashtabula with the Cleveland, Painesville & Ashtabula. The CP&E opened the thirty-mile stretch between Cleveland and Painesville on July 4, 1896, and opened an alternate Shore Line along Lakeshore Boulevard and Vine Street connecting Cleveland and Willoughby.

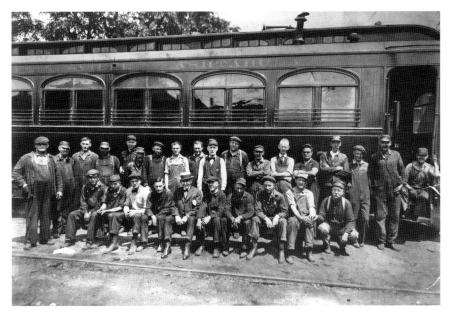

CP&A interurban employees. *Courtesy of Little Red Schoolhouse.*

The CP&E was owned by the Everett-Moore syndicate, led by Henry Everett and Edward Moore. According to the June 1988 *Lake County Historical Quarterly*, Everett was born in Cleveland in 1856, and his father, Dr. Azariah Everett, was president of the East Cleveland Railroad Company, one of the country's first successful electric railways. When Henry began working for the company at age eighteen, it sparked his interest in street railways.

Moore, born in Canal Dover, Ohio, in 1864, began his career as a teller in the banking house of Everette, Weddell & Company. His interest in streetcars began while he was working for the Nickel Plate Railroad and investing in the East Cleveland Railroad Company, where Everett was secretary-treasurer.

The two formed the Everett-Moore syndicate in 1891, which controlled traction systems in Ohio, Michigan, New York, West Virginia and Canada, along with telephone companies throughout the region. By 1904, the syndicate controlled over 1,500 miles of track in northeast Ohio and had invested in constructing and reconditioning several railway bridges.

As their company grew, so did their families. Moore married Louise Chamberlin, and they had five children. They had a town home in Cleveland's University Circle and built their country estate, Mooreland

Mansion, on property that once stretched from the site of Great Lakes Mall on Mentor Avenue to the Kirtland flats.

Everett married Josephine Pettengil, and they had three children, but one died in infancy. Everett built a country estate of four hundred acres, neighboring Moore's property, called Leo-Doro Farm (named after his children Leolyn and Dorothy), which is now Kirtland Country Club. Everett even had a private parlor car on the interurban named Josephine, after his wife. It was painted green and gold, with hand-carved mahogany, green draperies, an observation lounge and an office.

The interurban contributed greatly to the growth of Lake County. Because the interurban made possible an hour-and-a-half trip from Cleveland to Willoughby, it became more convenient to work in the city and live in the country. The interurban improved the flow of business, too, by allowing farmers to ship their produce and dairy products to Cleveland, and it transported shoppers to the famed downtown Cleveland stores.

The Shore Line's second stop into Lake County from Cuyahoga County was stop 144, Willoughbeach Park. The Everett-Moore syndicate owned the park and tried to develop it into another Cedar Point. It had a dance hall, several rides (including a carousel and auto coaster called the Jack Rabbit, in which auto owners could drive their cars up a steep incline and coast down the track), baseball fields and its own team, picnic areas and a bathing beach. Willoughbeach became a popular destination for church outings and company picnics and was promoted on billboards and in newspaper ads as far away as Buffalo and Detroit.

The interurban looped into the park in front of the main pavilion, and it once had a wreck at the entrance, caused during switching. (Interestingly, when the old wooden interurban trestle came down in Willoughby, to be replaced by a steel bridge, the timbers were taken to Willoughbeach Park and used to build a new dance hall.)

The year the Shore Line opened, the company acquired the Painesville, Fairport and Richmond Street Railway, which began operating in Painesville in 1893 via a line from Painesville to Fairport.

In 1900, the Everett-Moore syndicate opened a subsidiary to the CP&E, called the Cleveland, Painesville and Ashtabula, which extended twenty-seven miles east by 1904. According to *Northern Ohio's Interurbans*, the two routes drew thousands of passengers away from the New York Central and Nickel Plate lines heading in the same direction.

As cars grew in popularity, use of the interurbans declined. In January 1926, the CP&E sold its property to the Cleveland Electric Illuminating

CP&E wreck in front of Willoughbeach. *Courtesy of Willoughby Historical Society.*

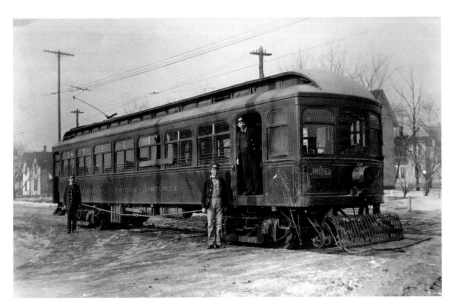

CP&A "Limited" trolley and crew in Willoughby, 1918. *Courtesy of Willoughby Historical Society.*

Company due to operating deficits of $100,000 a year. Within months, Willoughbeach Park, which relied on the interurban to bring people to the park, declared bankruptcy and was quickly overgrown by weeds.

A weak financial structure at the syndicate was also to blame for its closure, along with growing safety concerns among riders about the deteriorating bridges that the interurbans crawled across at five miles an hour, which were weak with age and swayed in the wind. In fact, a bridge did collapse in Fairport in 1918, injuring ten of the fifteen passengers on board.

In some cities along the route, there were other concerns. According to the 1988 *Lake County Historical Quarterly*, "[In] Perry residents complained that their village was being used as a dropping-off point for drunks and freeloaders that were picked up by the CP&A."

Downtown Willoughby was once a vital link for the CP&E, housing the headquarters and station, along with the railroad repair shop and powerhouse. As of September 28, 1948, according to a *News-Herald* article, some of the last rails of the interurban were embedded in the floor of the railroad shop building (which later became Willoughby Brewing Company).

In 1910, a new brick station had been built, replacing an old house. At the time, this new structure (now housing businesses Etc. on Erie and B. Legrand) dominated downtown Willoughby. It had offices upstairs, overseeing the shops, car yard, trestle and modern waiting rooms and baggage facilities downstairs. The building, originally located in what is now a parking lot,

Cleveland Painesville & Eastern (CP&E) interurban in front of original ticket office in downtown Willoughby, 1906. *Author's collection.*

Downtown Willoughby in 1927, during construction of buildings alongside the CP&E interurban ticket building. *Courtesy of Little Red Schoolhouse.*

was moved up to where it is today, and other buildings were constructed on either side.

By 1946, few remnants survived from the interurban. Rails were covered in asphalt on Erie Street, a few scattered stop signs were tacked to telephone poles along Vine Street, part of the concrete arch that marked the entrance to Willoughbeach remained and pieces of the defaced and crumbling concrete bridge clung to the walls of the Chagrin River valley, south of the Route 20 high-level bridge.

Stories of the interurban have been passed down through generations. Ann Dewald recalls her mother, Ruth Alexander, telling her she took the interurban from Willowick to Downtown Willoughby for school starting in sixth grade, because there wasn't enough room in the little Willowick schoolhouse, and attended Union High School until she graduated. She told Ann that on the way to school, the boys on the interurban sometimes disconnected the pole in the car that went up to the electrical wire, timing it as they went over a clay pit (likely linked to the Penfield brick company in Willoughby) around where Hardees is today on Vine Street. It took the driver about an hour to repair the connection, particularly challenging over a clay pit, which was long enough to be "good and late to school."

Railroads and Depots

The current railroads in Lake County (CSX) in the north and Norfolk Southern (NS) in the south have gone through many mergers and name changes through the years.

According to Tom Pescha of the Painesville Railroad Museum, the CSX tracks started as the CP&A, which merged with the Cleveland and Toledo Railroad to become Lake Shore Railroad Company in March 1869, then merged again several months later with the newly formed Lake Shore and Michigan Southern Railroad (LS-MS).

In 1914, the New York Central Railroad was formed by the consolidation of the LS-MS and ten other railroads. Consolidated Rail (Conrail) was formed in 1988 to take over many of the railroads, including the New York Central, and by 1997, CSX and NS had taken over Conrail.

Pescha goes on to say that the other tracks started out as the famed Nickel Plate Railroad (New York, Chicago and St. Louis Railroad), built in 1881. In 1964, it merged with Norfolk and Western Railroad (N&W), was taken over by Conrail and eventually became NS.

The Baltimore and Ohio (B&O) Lake Branch line from Grand River to Youngstown was removed in the 1980s, and now most of the line has been

Nickel Plate railroad bridge over the Chagrin River in Willoughby. *Courtesy of Willoughby Historical Society.*

Children standing in front of Nickel Plate railroad wreck. *Courtesy of Willoughby Historical Society.*

converted into rail trails, including Lake Metroparks Greenway Corridor linking Painesville, Painesville Township and Concord Township. Finally, the Fairport, Painesville and Eastern Railroad (FP&E) began in 1870 as a narrow-gauge line—the distance between the rail heads was 36 inches instead of the standard 56½ inches—that started in Fairport, serving the Diamond Shamrock company, and is now under NS control.

The railroad depots established at regular intervals along the lines were the center of activity in many Lake County towns, providing shelter, water and fuel for locomotives, repair services and, sometimes, transfer facilities with other lines.

According to *Railroad Depots of Northeast Ohio*, the typical depot was a frame or brick structure, with a waiting room on one end, a freight room on the other and an office with ticket counter in between. It was simply furnished with wooden benches and a potbelly stove. Before telephones, the depots connected the community with the outside world through the telegraph in their offices. Some larger communities had separate passenger and freight depots.

As the need for railroads declined, depots were often demolished or moved to serve another purpose. In 1919, Wickliffe had a depot that was still considered out in the country, and it stood until at least the 1970s.

Wickliffe LS&MS passenger depot, which was located east of Lloyd Road. *Courtesy of Tom Pescha/Painesville Railroad Museum.*

Men going off to war at the Painesville train depot, circa 1942. *Courtesy of Tom Pescha/ Painesville Railroad Museum.*

LS&MS maintained a small, enclosed passenger shelter at Reynolds Road. *Railroad Depots of Northeast Ohio* goes on to say, "Mentor was the site of the LS&MS greenhouse that supplied plants for the depot gardens along this stretch of the main line. Obviously, the gardens at Mentor's LS&MS depot were well kept and an enjoyable welcome to the city of all arriving by train.

In 1893, the LS&MS opened a new passenger depot at Painesville, which operated until 1971. It sat unused for years before the Western Reserve Railroad Association formed in 1997 to preserve the historic site, now the Painesville Railroad Museum.

Between Painesville and Perry, the LS&MS also maintained an enclosed, unmanned shelter at Lane into the 1930s, dating from 1870, with a standard freight house nearby, along with a small waiting shelter for the CP&E. None of these depots or shelters remain in Perry.

MYSTERY OF THE 1905 MENTOR TRAIN WRECK

On a late spring evening, June 21, 1905, travelers are winding down for the night on the esteemed LS&MS Twentieth Century Limited train. (The exclusive passenger train was the height of luxury and even believed to originate the phrase "red carpet treatment," because passengers boarded the train via a red carpet.)

Passengers gaze out the windows at the land speeding by as they rush forward on the fastest train in the world, traveling up to ninety-six miles an hour. Gentlemen gather in the buffet car for their final smoke of the night. Little do they know that their quiet evening is about to be shattered.

Night operator and agent C.J. Minor awaits the train at the Mentor Depot (which was located on Station Street, just east of Center Street behind what is now Deeker's Bar & Party Center). First, train number 10 passes through Mentor heading east at 8:35 p.m. A short while later, Minor heads out to check the track and signals before ducking back inside the freight depot to avoid the deafening roar and spray of debris of the Twentieth Century Flyer hurtling by.

The train approaches Mentor from the west at about seventy miles an hour. At 9:20 pm, it hits an open switch in front of the depot, jumping the track despite an emergency brake, jolting the passengers as it plows through the earth. The train, diverted from the main line, flips over atop the freight depot, twisting around to face the direction from which it had come, with the buffet car stacked on top of the engine.

Sixty-five to seventy passengers were aboard, spanning the buffet car, named the Missouri, which was the first car after the locomotive, followed by three Pullman cars (the Barbantio, Astolfo and Simla) and the fifth, a sleeper and observation car.

The wreckage caught on fire when the engine's boiler exploded, and the flames spread quickly through the wooden cars. Passengers trapped inside the buffet car didn't survive the scorching heat of the steam and boiling water pouring in, while the other four cars were hardly damaged. The surviving passengers and crew immediately began rescuing the injured.

Flames shot out of the freight depot, and Mentor residents who heard the crash hurried to the scene and formed a bucket brigade to put out the fire. Firemen struggled to reach the site with their hoses, so additional hoses were brought in from the nearby Mentor Knitting Mill (which was located in the Matchworks building), where some believe the ghosts of the wreck still roam today. Men worked with axes and crowbars, and some even bravely entered the burning wreckage to rescue those trapped inside. The fire raged for about five hours.

Cleveland industrialists Edward W. Moore and Horace Andrews, both heavily involved in the railway industry, arrived from their nearby summer homes to help with the rescue efforts. (Moore was co-owner of the CP&E, and Andrews was president and director of several railways, including the Cleveland Electric Railway Company.) Andrews was said to console his fatally injured friend, Charles H. Wellman, who gave him a message to deliver to his wife before he died.

Many of the women at the wreck cared for the injured passengers, including trained nurse Elizabeth Lynch, the first woman to arrive. Mattresses and bedding were brought from the train cars and nearby homes. Twenty minutes after a call was made to a doctor in Painesville, a train carrying doctors and additional residents arrived to help. Many of the injuries consisted of burns, so linseed oil, brought from a local paint shop, was applied to the wounds.

Just before midnight, a train arrived from Cleveland to take injured passengers to several hospitals. Nearly two dozen people were injured, and twenty died, including the engineer, in what is believed to be the deadliest accident in Mentor's history. It's also one of the city's greatest mysteries, because the cause of the accident is still unknown.

When the luxury train first ran in 1902, it took eighteen hours to go from Chicago to New York City's Grand Central Station, cutting down travel time by four hours. The New York Central Railroad was so confident in its timetable that it guaranteed passengers a one-dollar-per-hour reimbursement of their fifty-dollar one-way ticket for any delays along the way.

Some questioned whether the train's high speed caused it to skip the switch and crash, while others speculated it was behind schedule and trying to make up time. But news reports dispute some of those accusations.

A June 22, 1905 *Scranton Truth* article reads:

> *It is known that the locomotive in spite of its great speed took the switch properly and followed by the forward cars ran 150 feet on the sidetrack. At a point midway between the switch and the station the engine left the rails, plunged along the ties for 50 yards, where it turned end for end and fell and ploughed into the freight house.*

Sabotage was suspected, since evidence pointed to deliberate tampering of the switch. According to a June 23, 1905 Cleveland *Plain Dealer* article, a boy of about fourteen was seen carrying a lantern near the wreck about twenty minutes after the accident. When questioned, he said he had been down to the tracks to shut off the switch. However, his story didn't add up.

The *Scranton Truth* article continues,

> *General Manager Marshal, of the Lake Shore, said this morning that he found undisputable evidence that the switch had been thrown against the train and was locked open. It is impossible for a switch to be open and at the same time to show a white signal light unless the switch mechanism has been tampered with.*

Since there was nothing to show that the switch mechanism had indeed been tampered with, charges were never filed.

The wreck also drew crowds of curious sightseers and relic hunters, according to the *Plain Dealer*:

> *Hordes of workmen came and went, railway men dashed about directing the work of clearing, and everywhere were the people who had come from east and west, filled with curiosity to see the place where so many lives had been lost. The workmen had abandoned the pile of ashes and in it groped all sorts of people, with all sorts of implements. A pailful of jewels had been found in the wreckage and carried away, and all were eager to find something more. Umbrellas and sticks, or twisted bits of iron, were used by the more dainty.*

Others, down on their knees in the blackened dust, dug with both hands, reaching far down into the heap in search of possible treasure. And many as they scratched and dug, laughed and joked in their search, thoughtless of the men and women for whose possessions they were delving in that awful pile.

The original freight station, destroyed during the accident, was rebuilt, but the passenger depot across the tracks, at 8455 Station Street, has remained intact, although it has been modified since it became a restaurant.

GIRL IN BLUE

Another train tragedy remained a Lake County mystery for decades.

On Christmas Eve morning, 1933, a young woman, traveling alone, stepped off a Greyhound bus in Willoughby.

According to Cathi Weber's *Haunted Willoughby*, a man who was also stepping off noticed she seemed confused by her surroundings and asked if he could help her find a place to stay. She said she preferred to stay in a "tourist home" instead of a motel, and he escorted her to Mary Judd's boardinghouse on Second Street.

The next morning, the woman came down to breakfast fashionably dressed in a navy blue skirt and shoes, a white blouse, a floral-print scarf around her neck, a blue wool overcoat draped over her arm and a dark blue hat perched stylishly on her head.

Later she walked through a residential neighborhood, then through a wooded area.

"She was faced with the railroad tracks stretching out in the distance," writes Weber.

Suddenly barreling down the track at about sixty-five miles per hour, there was an eastbound flyer heading to New York. She dropped her suitcase as she sprinted toward the tracks. The engineer caught a blur of blue out of his peripheral vision, just time enough to make brief eye contact with the frantic woman. With a look of fear, she stared at him as she halted just inches from the speeding train. A glancing blow from the train sent her slight body hurtling through the air, landing on the gravel siding. Her short-lived life was tragically over. And the mysterious legend of the Girl in Blue was born.

She was about twenty-three years old, five feet four inches and 135 pounds, with strawberry blonde hair and hazel eyes, and she had nothing in her purse to identify her, only coins, a handkerchief, makeup and small trinkets.

She became known simply as the Girl in Blue. Although they tried, the townspeople were unable to identify her, so they came together to give her a proper burial. A resident donated a plot in the Willoughby cemetery, the owner of a local funeral home provided a funeral and the community donated money to pay for a beautifully etched gravestone with this inscription:

Girl in Blue
Killed by a train
December 24, 1933
Unknown but not forgotten

For years, people have left flowers and coins on her grave, and the city even created a fund to ensure geraniums are planted on her grave every year.

Decades later, in 1993, the *News-Herald* ran an article on the sixtieth anniversary of her death. Edward Sekerak, a real estate broker near Corry, Pennsylvania, just happened to read it, and he recalled the sale of the Klimczak family farm, in 1985. He and his wife, Lauri Remington-Sekerak, owner of a property and title research business, uncovered court documents that led to the discovery that the Girl in Blue was named Josephine Klimczak. Known as Sophie by her family, she was one of nine children of Jacob and Catherine Klimczak, who had owned a one-hundred-acre farm in Warren County, Pennsylvania. To sell the estate, her brother Leo filed a signed affidavit in 1985, stating Josephine was "killed in an accident in Willoughby, Ohio, on December 24, 1933; was unmarried; had not been identified until after the death of her father, Jacob Klimczak (1934); and was buried as the 'Girl in Blue' following her accidental death."

Residents of Willoughby and the surrounding communities were elated to hear that the Girl in Blue had finally been identified, and a second gravestone was added with her full name.

Many people still visit her grave today, and it is a stop on the Willoughby "Ghost Walk," where some claim to have seen a blue orb floating near her grave.

WILLOUGHBY VIADUCT

In 1916, motivated by the stalemate on the ground in Europe during World War I, the federal government established a system of highways to aid in national defense. Existing roads were designated as U.S. highways, and other roads were improved and assigned state route numbers, like Mentor and Euclid Avenue, which became part of U.S. Route 20.

In 1921, the Willoughby Viaduct was built over the Chagrin River, connecting the two roads, which helped the city grow. It opened with much fanfare as people lined up on either side of the bridge for the festivities. Euclid-Chardon Road, designated as U.S. Route 6, was the only other U.S. highway in the county.

VULCAN CARS

A.R. Marsh started a factory in Painesville to build automobiles in 1913, and for two years, Painesville was the home of the "World's Greatest Light Car" (according to its advertisements).

The two-passenger Speedster cost $750 to buy in 1913, and the five-passenger Touring car was $850, but just a year later, as additional accessories were added, each car cost $850. Once ignition and lighting systems were added, along with a Westinghouse generator, the price ranged from $912 to $975.

The selling points included: "Built strong and durable, pleasing and graceful lines, will turn in 15 feet radius, silent in its action, and powerful and speedy." The radiator emblem was a black upside-down triangle with a gold clenched fist, holding lightning bolts shooting out horizontally on either side. "Vulcan Mfg Co Painesville Ohio" was written below.

Some lucky teenage boys even got to test drive the Vulcan from seven o'clock in the morning to five o'clock in the afternoon in the summer months, checking for performance of the chassis. (Their favorite obstacles were said to be Hogsback Hill in Concord Township and Main Street Hill in Painesville).

By 1915, inefficiency and poor management had taken their toll on the company, and it went bankrupt.

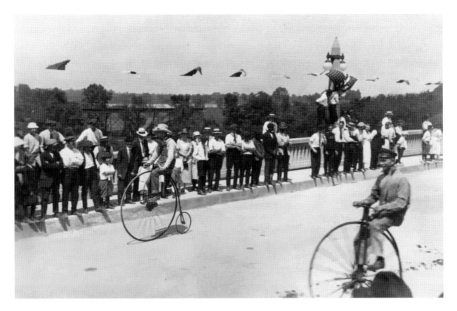

Above: Bicyclists in Willoughby viaduct dedication parade, June 29, 1921. *Courtesy of Willoughby Historical Society.*

Left: Vulcan car ad in 1913 *Motor Magazine. Courtesy of Bill Smith.*

Ben Hur

For an even shorter time span, Ben Hur Motor Company produced a clover-leaf roadster at a factory in Willoughby. This was a continuation of the Allen automobile, created by L.L. Allen, who was hoping that a name change would help increase sales. It debuted in 1917, and in February, Allen announced that he had shipped thirty automobiles and was making five to ten a week, although the factory had the capacity to produce up to twenty cars a day. By May, the company had begun shutting down.

East Shore Cab

In the 1940s, East Shore Cab Company opened on Euclid Avenue, in Wickliffe, next to what was once a restaurant called Sonny's Side of the Street. The cab company was run by brothers Louis and Theodore Dellafiora, until Louis married his wife, Lois, in 1948, and she began running the business, too. "She was always a part of it while growing up, as was I," says their daughter Karen Sendek. "Dad taught me how to how to maintain a car,

Lois and Louis Dallafiora, owners of Eastshore Cab, circa late 1940s/early '50s. *Courtesy of Karen Sendek.*

didn't want me on the side of the road with a flat." A 1978 *News-Herald* article states that Lois served as "dispatcher, officer organizer, and all-around handyman" since the business opened.

Whether they needed a ride to the market, office or beauty parlor, Eastlake housewives, businessmen and senior citizens depended on East Shore Cab.

Sendek says that in the 1950s, the company moved to what is now the northeast corner of Ohio State Route 91. When Lois's husband, Louis, died in 1964, she was left to run the whole business on her own, uncommon for a woman at the time.

"I never minded the work because we made so many friends," Lois explains in the *News-Herald* article. "They were the regulars who would call for a taxi the same time each day."

A year later, she remarried Thomas Hickman, who was busy working twelve- to fourteen-hour days as manager of the Arco service station on East 354th and Vine Street in Eastlake, so she continued running the business.

"The taxi business just doesn't pay for anybody who has to rely on it for their only income," Lois said. "If someone decided to run the business for a second income, they could make it." And she did make it for years, but over time, taxis were no longer as in demand as they once were, as many families began owning more than one car.

After three decades, Lois and her husband, Thomas, decided the "skimpy profits" and the constant battle with the rising cost of gasoline, oil and repairs weren't worth the time to keep the business running, and they decided to close shop.

Chapter 5

BEYOND THE GRISTMILL

INDUSTRY IN THE 1800s–1900s

Agriculture has always been an important part of Lake County. Due
to its proximity to Lake Erie, it has a defined nursery belt on its
eastern side, from Madison to Mentor, that stays warmer in the fall
and is protected against early frosts in the spring.

In 1854, Storrs & Harrison Company nursery in Painesville became the
largest department nursery in the world, and many other successful nurseries
followed. At one time, Mentor, which lies within the nursery belt, was known
as the "Rose Capital of the Nation," with over a dozen large rose growers
producing five million plants a year at its peak.

Debonne Vineyards, in Madison Township, is the largest estate winery in
Ohio and has grown steadily since it opened in the 1970s. But the Grand
River valley isn't the only place grapes have been grown. The Shakers had
a large vineyard that stretched across what is now Wickliffe and Willowick,
along Worden Road. *A History of Kirtland, Ohio* says some Kirtlanders even
played a role in Prohibition by selling grapes to illegal manufacturers, making
a pretty good profit, since grape selling wasn't illegal.

Lillie Tryon Curtis, who grew up in Waite Hill in the 1800s, remembered
there was always an abundant variety of apples in her family's cellar:

> *Every evening when the chores were all done and the family gathered around
> the bright fire, father would get a candle and "take a look down the cellar
> to see how the apples are keeping." Bringing up a big dish of those bright-
> colored apples, he would sit down with a sharp knife, on the point of which he
> would pass each apple in turn leaving the juicy fruit neatly pared, cored, and*

quartered. "An apple a day keeps the doctor away," he said, and there was seldom the need for a physician at the Tryon house, where fruit abounded and was freely eaten. All this made the hard work more tolerable, even pleasant.

PERRY ONION FIELDS

In the late 1800s, Nelson House, in Perry, was the largest cider and vinegar mill in northern Ohio, but the region was also known for its onions. It was one of our nation's greatest onion producers, thanks to the fine, almost black soil, called muck, that was ideal for growing.

According to Mary L. Platko's *A Little Bit of Perry History*, Lake County was the first in the state to produce onions for shipment, and at one time more onions were raised in Lake County per acre than any other county statewide: 848,066 bushels in 1901.

James McVitty did particularly well as an onion farmer, and his success lingered years later when an antique shop named the Onion Shoppe opened

"Harvesting a profitable crop of [giant] onions," 1909. *Courtesy of Madison Historical Society.*

Onion shed located in the Madison railroad district. Years ago, onions were shipped all over the country from Madison distributor A.N. Benjamin Produce, on Lake Street. *Courtesy of Madison Historical Society.*

across from the Queen Anne–style home he had built and lived in on Main Street in Perry Village.

At one point, this burgeoning crop was given the name the Perry Rose, which, according to local legend, may have originated from travelers passing through Perry who smelled the aroma of the many onion fields. Onions were stored in sheds throughout Perry and neighboring Madison and shipped by railroad.

Remnants of these early onion crops are believed to remain throughout Perry today in the form of wild onions.

DAIRIES

In the mid-nineteenth century, at the height of dairy farming, the Western Reserve was known as Cheesedom. In fact, in 1847, more than 1 million pounds of cheese and nearly 309,000 pounds of butter were exported from Fairport. A group of men formed an association called the Lake County Milk Company, and according to *History of Geauga and Lake Counties, Ohio, 1798–1878*, the association built two cheese factories in Willoughby over a ten-year span.

By 1876, cheese production had dropped, but milk and cream were sent to Cleveland and New York by the Lake Shore Railroad, and dairying remained an important part of the county's economy for years. Ice cream shops like Frank Smith Ice Cream Parlor, which was a popular place to stop in Mentor in the 1920s, could be found throughout the region.

Getting milk delivered to your house by a milkman is a thing of the past, but many old homes still have an exterior latched door where bottles of cold milk, cheese and butter were placed. Others recall milk being delivered in insulated aluminum boxes on the front porch. For many, the memories of a visit from the milkman remain vivid: the fresh, cold bottles; peeling back the aluminum foil seal to reveal a layer of fresh cream on the top of the milk.

According to James Naughton's book, *70 Years of Living in Kirtland*, there were three dairy farms in Kirtland in 1937, until after World War II. Hilltop Farms, on Billings Road, delivered milk for just ten cents for a two-quart bucket. McFarland's Dairy, on Joseph Street, sold milk to Euclid Race Dairy. The largest dairy was on Chillicothe Road at the Morley House, run by Maynard Freshley.

Lynn Carlton (*on stool*) and Mary Muffett (*at counter*) at Frank Smith Ice Cream Parlor in Mentor, 1923. *Courtesy of Lynn Carlton.*

According to Naughton, they had two large barns and four milk trucks that peddled milk in the Cleveland Heights area. Businessman and philanthropist Leonard Hanna, who lived at Hilo Farm in Kirtland Hills, gave Mr. Freshley tickets to a Cleveland Indians baseball game at the old League Park.

"And Mr. Freshley gave the four milk trucks to take us kids to the ball game," Naughton continues. "Seeing Babe Ruth, Lou Gehrig, Joe DiMaggio, Bob Feller, Hal Trosky and Joe Vosmik, a Kirtland resident, was really a great thrill."

In Fairport Harbor, North Star Dairy, on Eagle Street from 1935 through the 1960s, delivered milk right to residents' doors. And in Painesville, Reed Sunshine Dairy Company, Riggs Countryside Dairy, Maple Brook Dairy and Lockie-Lee Dairy were all well-known dairies in the early- to mid-twentieth century.

LOCKIE-LEE DAIRY

Linda (Loxterman) Jones had an in when it came to ice cream, since her dad, Lawrence Loxterman, was the president of Lockie-Lee Dairy.

Brothers Lawrence G., John "Jack," Andrew "Andy" and William "Bill" Loxterman and Lee Dietrich started Lockie-Lee Dairy in the late 1940s. Linda says in the beginning they all did pretty much everything, including delivering the bottles of milk and dairy products.

Linda's dad grew up in a large family in Fairport, the tenth of eleven children. Before starting Lockie-Lee, he was in the navy, and his brothers worked for Reed Sunshine Dairy in the 1940s. When they became incorporated, the name Lockie-Lee came from Lockie, Lawrence's (and possibly the other brothers') nickname, and Lee, their dairy partner.

Linda remembers her dad telling her the company started in Mentor, in an old barn, but she only remembers it being on Chester Street in Painesville. The company delivered milk and dairy products not only to homes but also to most of the schools in the area. In the 1960s, they saw an opportunity to seize a growing market that would give them another outlet to sell their products, and they bought the Northeast Ohio Convenient Food Mart franchise.

The company grew from a little mom-and-pop business into one that, in its heyday, had 140 stores in the region. Lockie-Lee even had a restaurant in the 1950s, at the corner of State and Main Streets, in the building that became home to Toyland. "My mom worked there. Some of my aunts

Left: Lawrence G. Loxterman, president of Lockie-Lee Dairy, holding his daughter Linda Loxterman Jones in 1950. *Courtesy of Linda Loxterman Jones.*

Right: Lawrence G. Loxterman in front of a Lockie-Lee Dairy truck in the 1950s. *Courtesy of Linda Loxterman Jones.*

worked there, and mom would bring me [as a baby] and I would just sit there all day and smile at the customers," recalls Linda.

Linda said that through the years, one of things that always stuck out was her dad's work ethic; he did it all and wasn't afraid to work hard. Her mom once told her that she remembered seeing him outside in a shirt and tie laying brick while they were adding on to the building. "He was proud of what he had done; basically they built it from nothing, and yet my dad stayed true to his roots," says Linda. "He didn't have much growing up as a family with eleven kids. He was careful with how he spent money and spent it wisely."

Lockie-Lee also employed a lot of people from the community, and school classes enjoyed going to the processing plant for tours. Linda says they got the milk from local farmers and processed it on Chester Street, with machines bottling and capping the milk.

Linda, the oldest of three siblings, remembers that when she and her family lived in Madison through the early 1960s, they visited her grandparents Jim and Hilda Hine in Wickliffe on Saturdays. (The Hines lived near the drive-in theater and could see the screen from their backyard, so Jim built a screened-in porch behind the garage with chairs to watch the movies without sound.) Linda said they had only one car, so her mom, Pearl, dropped off her dad at the dairy on the way and picked him up on the way back. She remembers seeing her dad sitting at the ice cream machine when they stopped to pick him up, filling empty cartons.

"I can remember him making cherry vanilla, and some gallons got more cherries than others because it depended on how much he was talking," laughs Linda. "There was always a little left in the machine, and he would put it in cups, and we would have cups of fresh soft ice cream."

In the early 1990s, the owners sold Lockie-Lee to Dairymans and retired.

Over the years, glass milk bottles and Lockie-Lee memorabilia have become quite collectible. In fact, Linda collects Lockie-Lee items for her personal collection and to pass down to her daughters. It seems there may have been many more bottles on the market had they not been thrown away when the dairy converted from glass milk bottles to paper cartons. Linda's brother remembers dumping them by the truckload.

Besides the rarity of the items, it's the nostalgia for a simpler time that draws people to the Lockie-Lee name.

"The personal touch to it—people knew their milkman," says Linda. "The milkman would come to your house, he would make recommendations: 'Do you need any cottage cheese today? How are you doing on ice cream?' It was very personal, and that is something we've lost today."

BRICK MANUFACTURERS

J.W. Penfield Brick and Tile Machine Company

A Penfield brick, 1890s. *Courtesy of Willoughby Historical Society.*

Brick manufacturers were an important part of developing Lake County, as they allowed roads to be built.

James W. Penfield arrived in Willoughby Township with his family in 1834 and helped on their family farm on the site of Pine Ridge Country Club, where his father, Wakeman Penfield, started a brick

American Clay Machinery Company, Willoughby. *Courtesy of Little Red Schoolhouse.*

factory. According to *Here Is Ohio's Lake County*, that's where he came up with the idea that one of the great needs of the country's farmlands was to be able to drain the soil, so he designed machinery to manufacture drain tiles. He quickly realized the same machinery could be used to manufacture bricks, which were mainly made by hand up to that point.

J.W. married Elsie Ferguson in 1850, and they had three daughters, Glendora, Edith and Gertrude, and a son, Raymond. Following in his father's footsteps, J.W. started a brick company called J.W. Penfield and Son on Ridge Road, which moved close to the river, near the tracks, and became known as J.W. Penfield Brick and Tile Machine Company. It made tiles and bricks and supplied other factories with the machinery to make their own tiles and bricks, which made Penfield a pioneer and leader in the development of the machine-building industry. Not only did Penfield bricks help build many of Cleveland's most well-known structures, but Penfield's line of machinery could be found throughout the country as well.

In the early 1870s, Penfield's machine shop, foundry and factory took up a large section of land at the east end of the Pelton Street Bridge in Willoughby. Joseph Boyce, who ran the Boyce Mill nearby on the Chagrin River, also joined his brick factory. According to documents found in the Willoughby Historical Society archives, "That nearby bridge was the only way through town, after passing the site and the bridge and then over the tracks and into Willoughby. President Garfield passed that way as he came from Mentor to Willoughby."

J.W. lived with his family in a Victorian mansion on the corner of Erie Street and Glenn Avenue in downtown Willoughby. In fact, Glenn Avenue was named after his daughter Glendora, who became an accomplished singer. (The CP&E terminal building was on the other side of the mansion.)

In 1887, J.W.'s daughter Gertrude married Frank W. Seiberling of Akron in their Willoughby home on Erie Street and Glen Avenue (Seiberling founded Goodyear Rubber Company twelve years later and built Stan Hywet mansion in Akron).

The Penfield company became internationally known for manufacturing tube and ball mills for pulverizing Portland cement. J.W.'s son, Raymond, and his nephew, Louis W. Penfield (who later became mayor from 1892 to 1894), helped run the company.

When J.W. passed away in 1897, his home became the home and office of noted Willoughby physician Dr. Thomas Moore.

According to the Willoughby Historical Society archives, Penfield Brick consolidated with the Frey-Sheckler Company of Bucyrus, and in 1905, the name changed to the American Clay Machinery Company. Hundreds of people were employed at both locations. Many local roads were paved with American Clay's red bricks, including Erie Street in Willoughby in 1911 and Mentor Avenue, once called the worst road in the county, in 1915.

During World War I, Penfield's company began manufacturing shell casings, and the business expanded to two additional plants in Illinois and Mansfield, but when the war ended, they weren't needed. Hundreds of people lost their jobs when the plant closed in 1926.

Wickliffe Brick Plant

In 1889, the Cleveland Brick Company manufactured its first brick in Wickliffe. According to a March 15, 1889 *Willoughby Independent* article, "The machinery runs like clockwork; they run very slowly and two men were kept busy taking the brick from the press. They run out 3,000 in a couple of hours. The company has a number of large contracts to fill and will be kept busy from now on."

By 1892, the name changed to the Buckeye Brick and Tile Works Company, producing twenty-five thousand bricks a day, with a nearby boardinghouse for employees. According to the Wickliffe Historical Society's winter 2009 newsletter, when the railroads were built farther east, a colony of Irish families settled in the vicinity of the tracks, and the area became known as Irish Town.

The brickyard was affected by the depression of 1929 and stopped operating. In 1932, it reopened again, this time under the ownership of Euclid Shale Brick Company, but closed again due to poor economic conditions. The deep pit left by the brickyard on the Wickliffe/Euclid border, where blue shale was removed to grind into powder and make bricks, was used as a garbage dump for both cities for many years. It was closed after the clothes of a man who was dumping garbage at the site caught on fire, and he died nine days later.

LAKE SHORE NITROGLYCERINE COMPANY

In the late 1860s, a nitroglycerine plant was built in Fairport Harbor, where the Grand River meets Lake Erie. A 1972 *Plain Dealer* article says the Lake Shore Nitroglycerine Company was established to meet the demands for explosives in the copper country of upper Michigan. Nitroglycerine was a predecessor to dynamite, which is a more stable product, made by treating glycerine with concentrated nitric and sulphuric acids. Nitroglycerine was known for detonating unexpectedly, and it did so when a ship carrying a large cargo of it blew up off the coast of Panama. So, when the industry came to Fairport, there was opposition, led by lighthouse keeper George Rogers, whose home was closest to the site. "From what they could learn of nitroglycerine, Fairporters concluded that the plant, as a place to work, would not be conducive to long life and that job termination was likely to be extremely sudden."

The owners insisted they were taking the precaution of separating their facilities by placing the manufacturing operation on the east, or village, side of the river and two storage magazines on the west bank.

Residents were told the quantity of material being processed wasn't enough to cause an accident. However, the owners of the company, J.H. King, C.M. Wheeler and H. Hinkley, didn't live in Fairport but in Mentor and Painesville.

On September 10, 1870, a warm, late summer evening, a large explosion and a brilliant flash rang out, with heavy reverberations that "rattled windows, upset chinaware and brought a chorus of protesting howls from the canine population."

Residents hurried into the streets as news flew across town that the Lake Shore Nitroglycerine plant had exploded (containing about two thousand pounds of nitroglycerin).

The *Painesville Telegraph* reads:

> *A rush was made to the livery stables, and soon everything in the shape of horses and carriages were loaded and on their way to the scene of the explosion.…They found the whole population out, under the greatest excitement. All was confusion and terror. It was ascertained that one of the magazines across the river had exploded.…A hole to the depth of fifteen feet had been blown in the dirt and sand. A large magazine, nearby, strange as it may seem, did not explode. No one was injured, but considerable damage was done to the buildings in Fairport. Doors were burst open, windows smashed and houses badly shaken.*

Rogers was furious and led a group of citizens to confront the officials at the plant, threatening mob violence if they resumed operations.

The *Telegraph* reacted:

> *As it is the people of Fairport are very much excited and incensed against the Glycerine Company.…While we regret this state of things, and hope that there may be no violence, we yet feel that the citizens of Fairport have a right to demand that their lives and property be protected. But in this there is a right way and a wrong way, a good way and a bad way. A mob spirit is always a dangerous element in a community. It is never reasonable, and once started, it knows no bounds.*

Plant officials insisted none of their employees had been near the magazine for days, implying a disgruntled townsman triggered the explosion. But the company paid for home repairs and promised to rebuild magazines completely underground to buffer any potential future explosions.

Some families moved away, but the tempers of most in the community cooled. That is, until a much larger explosion at 4:45 p.m. on November 1, forty-four days later.

"And this time the explosion made the previous blast seem like a balmy summer zephyr or the pop of a champagne cork," reads the *Plain Dealer*. "This time all of the estimated 16,000 pounds of nitroglycerine stored in both magazines went up in one stupendous and catastrophic boom."

An eyewitness on the east bank of the river was looking across at the magazines at the time of the blast. He recognized four men at work: Michael Malone was digging the foundation pit for a third magazine; Pat Scribner and Edward Duncan were ferrying "frozen" stock from the magazines across the river to the processing buildings; Nelson Malone (Michael's son) was pouring liquid into cans for shipment inside one of the magazines.

"The witness recalled seeing Scribner and Duncan walking from the magazines toward the river when they suddenly disappeared, vanishing, he dazedly recounted, 'like the flame of a candle being snuffed out.'" A half second later, the anonymous witness was knocked unconscious by the blast but survived and vaguely recalled being bounced up and down by a series of intense reverberations.

A Painesville resident saw a brilliant flash in the north followed by a towering column of flame and a huge cloud of blood-red smoke that he said appeared to extend two miles high. He, too, was knocked over seconds later.

The shockwaves extended across Lake Erie and to Buffalo, New York, 150 miles away, where telegrams were dispatched to Cleveland asking if there had been an earthquake. Cows in Perry were thrown to their knees, and cups and plates in Geneva were jarred from shelves.

Fairport itself was said to be utter devastation.

> *First arrivals on the scene, peering through a haze of dust, were appalled. The entire population had taken to the streets, seemingly crazed. The concussion had been so great as to affect minds. Grown men, for no apparent reason, were fighting and scuffling. Women were weeping, screaming, and wrestling with each other. Children ran about, terrified.*

The streets were covered in bricks and wood torn from homes. It was cold, and nearly every chimney in town had been destroyed, so fires couldn't be built. Likely spurred by a rumor that over one thousand pounds of explosives were still being processed on the site, people began walking to Painesville for shelter.

Rogers's wife, who had been sick in bed, was hit by a door flying across the room. He was furious about the explosion and, undaunted by the rumor of more explosives, was said to have started swinging a sledgehammer at what was left of the production machinery at the plant. He was still hammering when officials arrived. (Rogers was later issued a warrant charging him with destruction of property but was acquitted after a four-day legal battle.)

One of the plant owners, J.H. King, was said to have apologized to the locals and paid for damages.

Ten days after the explosion, the nitroglycerine company began dismantling its factory, with a plan to move it where people's lives and properties wouldn't be endangered.

Ohio Rubber Company

Sarah Irish discovered a piece of Lake County history while removing carpet from her bedroom in Auburn, Michigan: an Ohio Rubber Company ad in the September 12, 1943 *Detroit Sunday Times*. "It was perfectly preserved under layers of carpet and vintage linoleum," said Irish. "It was found with dozens of other newspapers and magazines, all dating from the early 1940s." The full-page ad reads: "Tank tracks made by The Ohio Rubber Company are helping our armored divisions smash thru to victory. On all fronts, on land, at sea, and in the air, ORCO products are in action to help with this war."

The Willoughby building occupied by the Ohio Rubber Company perhaps had as many layers as that floor in Michigan. It manufactured not only rubber, used in World War II, but also automobiles and even poison gas. The latter was produced without residents in the quiet community of Willoughby realizing that a plant making a destructive chemical weapon was right at their doorsteps.

During World War I, poisonous gas was a weapon that could reach into the trenches in a way no other weapon could. When the United States entered the war in April 1917, a new, even deadlier gas was developed: lewisite. The methyl gas wasn't a gas at all. *Here Is Ohio's Lake County* says it was an oily liquid that smelled like geranium blossoms and was said to be seventy-two

OHIO RUBBER COMPANY   WILLOUGHBY, OHIO.   W6

Postcard of the Ohio Rubber Company in Willoughby. *Author's collection*.

times more deadly than mustard gas; even a small exposure could lead to death within minutes.

In the summer of 1918, the U.S. Army began manufacturing chemical weapons, including mustard and chlorine gases, to use against the Germans in World War I. The development division of the Chemical Warfare Services headquarters moved from Washington D.C. to Nela Park in Cleveland.

According to Jeffrey Frischkorn in the *News-Herald*, "Appropriately later called 'the Manhattan Project of World War I,' the lewisite program had components in several locations, including Willoughby. The Army believed the town's remoteness would keep it from the eyes of German spies and too-inquisitive newspaper reporters."

More than one hundred soldiers came to the former Ben Hur Motor Company automobile factory in Willoughby that summer and fall to work at the plant. "Working quickly, they labored for months under a constant threat of death more imminent than if they had been on the front lines."

Nathan A. Simpson served in 1918 with the "Nifty Nine and Briggs" platoon. He and his fellow soldiers arrived from all over and gathered at the Cleveland YMCA, believing they would be sent to the General Electric Company. However, as Simpson recalled in *Here Is Ohio's Lake County*, they were told to board a trolley and travel east to a building in Willoughby. "The conductor said, 'You know what? There is something mighty odd about the town of Willoughby. I have taken more than 100 GIs out there and NEVER BROUGHT ANY BACK!'"

The GIs never left until November 1918, and the production of gas was never mentioned inside or outside of the plant. If anyone asked, the men said they were working on a formula to improve rubber for the army, which was believable, considering the unpleasant smells coming from the plant. Although their mission was secretive, the troops were regularly seen out in town, eating breakfast and dinner at local restaurants and diners and attending socials at Andrews Institute for Girls (Andrews Osborne Academy).

The plant included several acres, surrounded by barbed wire, and by November 1918, it's believed it was producing ten to twenty tons of methyl gas a day. The Chemical Warfare Division was hoping to have three thousand tons of lewisite by spring of 1919 to use in a bombardment along the European front from the Alps to the English Channel. The war ended before the gas could be used, so the gas produced in Willoughby was said to have been transported by train to Baltimore, Maryland, and dumped far out into the Atlantic Ocean. According to Frischkorn:

> *Other accounts say the stuff was already aboard a ship headed for Europe. When news of the armistice reached the vessel, the transport and its poisonous cargo were sunk somewhere in the North Atlantic. However, as a reporter for The News-Herald in 2002 and conducting research for a story on this project, I spoke with one local person who said his late father told a tale of helping load casks of materiel onto a vessel which made its way out of the Chagrin River and into Lake Erie. There, the canisters were shoved overboard, the person's father said.*

Some say tanks of gas were found in an elevator shaft when installations were made at the Ohio Rubber Company and wonder whether lewisite components were buried at the site. Once, in 1957, up to fifty-seven bottles of possible lewisite were found and then dealt with by army chemical weapons disposal experts.

Remarkably, considering how volatile the gas they were producing was, not one serviceman died at the facility.

In 1919, only weeks after the last troops left the facility, the property was sold, and Buckeye Rubber Company (later Ohio Rubber Company) opened in the plant; it became one of the largest employers in the county. It closed in the early 1990s, but many have memories of working there or of family members who made their livelihood at the site.

Rick Ziemak grew up in Willoughby in the 1950s through '70s, and his grandfather Stanley Ziemak worked on the presses for several decades. Rick remembers him playing Santa at Ohio Rubber Christmas parties at the Vine theater during the '50s. "I remember the theater being packed with kids of all ages," Rick recalls.

Rick says his uncle Bill told him that Ohio Rubber used to have a summer picnic at Mentor Beach Park, and his grandpa once dressed up in full Indian wardrobe in a parade there.

The water tower used for the plant is still visible from Vine Street, with "DeMilta" written across it, a remnant reminding us of what could have been an extremely deadly contribution to the "war to end all wars."

INNS AND TAVERNS

The Bates Tavern

The Bates Tavern, owned by Ezra Bates, was located at the corner of Paine and Leroy Center Roads, across from Leroy Town Hall. Lori Watson, treasurer of the Leroy Heritage Association, says the tavern was built by master builder Jonathan Goldsmith around 1820 and was one of the earliest homes in Leroy.

1921 advertisement for the Leroy Grange Fair, which was held at the Bates Tavern. *Courtesy of the Leroy Heritage Association.*

Ezra, among the earliest settlers, moved to the area with his parents from Massachusetts in 1809, and his father, Benjamin, purchased the lot the tavern would stand on. The Bates family not only lived at the tavern but also hosted many travelers in the early years and held parties; the establishment served as a tavern, school, meeting place and ballroom. It's unknown whether it was the kind of place visitors just stopped for a drink or a meal or even stayed a week. Early township records show many trustee meetings were held there because the Town Hall wasn't built across the street until 1847.

The Bates Tavern, located in Leroy, in the late 1800s/early 1900s. *Courtesy of the Leroy Heritage Association.*

The Leroy Grange Fair was also held at the tavern. An advertisement dating from the early 1900s tries to lure visitors to the fair with promises of "field sports, fine prizes, a baby show" (perhaps along the lines of cutest or largest baby) and an "old-fashioned chicken pie dinner" for seventy-five cents. "Next to county fair in importance." General admission was just fifteen cents, and the Middlefield Orchestra was scheduled to play at the event.

The Bates Tavern was an important gathering place for the community for many years until it was demolished in 1936.

The Kingsley Hotel

In Willoughby's early days, inns and taverns were very popular due to the stagecoaches coming through the area. An undated newspaper article written by local historian, author, Andrews School trustee and Lake County treasurer Frank N. Shankland says,

> *In the early days of Willoughby, the only means of transportation was the stagecoach, which was used to come in from the east on Mentor Avenue, past the Daniel Brothers Coal Yard, and the Nickle Plate and New York*

Central rights of way, past the Browning plant, over the Chagrin River on a ford, and up the hill onto Erie Street, thence to Cleveland via Euclid Avenue, Glenn Avenue and the high-level bridge had not been heard of.

The stagecoaches stopped at the Zebra Stage Coach House (now the site of Willoughby Coal). The clapboards were painted alternating light green, yellow and white, giving them a zebralike appearance. Another popular stop was the Chagrin Tavern, which stood on the southeast corner of Erie Street and East Spaulding, along with Phelps Old Tavern, on the south side of Euclid Avenue (across from the site that was Cook Cleland's Airport, behind Dunkin' Donuts).

The Kingsley was one of the most well-known inns, beginning as the small wooden home of Hannah Ingersoll, built after the Civil War. The front porch contained her millinery (hats and headwear) store, which was the only one in town. It was attached to a brick building called the Powell House, which was a small hotel and was later bought by Willoughby merchant Frank L. Gibbons. He built a three-story addition, cleared a lot in the rear for a livery stable and renamed it Gibbons House.

In 1896, the property changed hands again, and it became the Kingsley Hotel, with a dining room and third-floor ballroom for dances. But perhaps the Kingsley's notoriety is due to its tragic past.

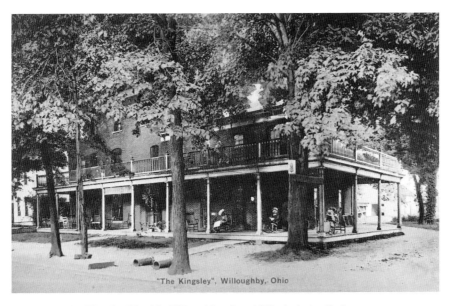

Postcard of the Kingsley Hotel in Willoughby, circa 1905. *Author's collection.*

In the early 1900s, Charles P. Corlett and his wife had been living at the Kingsley for nearly four years. "She was known about town as a woman fond of expensive clothing and a gay life, but caring little for local society, while he was a clever man of affairs and more reserved in tastes," reads the June 12, 1908 *Willoughby Independent*. "For some time Corlett had suspected undue friendliness by his wife toward other men, and their quarrels were not infrequent."

Corlett was known to go "into the city" (presumably Cleveland) each day, but he returned early on the day of the tragedy, at two o'clock, and went to his rooms on the first floor. "Sometime later Corlett appeared and asked for ice water, saying his wife was very ill. It should be here added that this sickness was caused by taking four tablets of corrosive sublimate, no doubt with suicidal intent."

Dr. Moore, who lived and had his office on the corner of Glenn Avenue and Erie Street, was called and was able to counter the effects of the deadly poison. Nothing more was heard from the couple that afternoon/evening until shots were fired. When E.H. Tryon, the hotel proprietor, fled his office and entered their room, he found the couple dead, with a revolver still clutched in the husband's hands. Corlett was forty-two years old, and his wife was thirty-five.

The Kingsley sat across from Third Street on the east side of Erie Street near where Sage Karma Kitchen is now. It was destroyed by fire in 1918.

FIRE IN FAIRPORT

Fires were common at the turn of the century. The McCrone House, on the southeast corner of Second and Water Streets in Fairport Harbor, was one of fourteen establishments destroyed during a major fire in 1890.

The Arlington Hotel, built in 1889 on the corner of Third and High Streets, was destroyed by a fire in 1931. It had a bar inside, which made it one of twenty-eight saloons in Fairport in 1901, according to tax receipts. (Fairport establishments alone made up more than half of the fifty-two saloons in Lake County that year.) *Fairport Harbor*, by the Fairport Harbor Historical Society, reads: "It was said that little water was drunk on Water Street in its early days."

According to Lee Silvi's account in a 2020 Fairport Harbor Historical Society newsletter, a fire ripped through Toubman's, the "Big Store"—as it was preparing to be demolished—on the southeast corner of Fourth and High Streets. Toubman's opened in 1901 and closed in the '70s.

The cause was suspicious. Silvi, who was a Fairport Harbor fire lieutenant, recalls that someone contacted the station the evening before the fire, saying "if" the building should catch fire before it was demolished, the firefighters shouldn't go in, because structural supports had been cut in the demolition process to make it easier to knock down. Within twenty-four hours, a mystery fire broke out.

When firefighters arrived, within three minutes of the alarm, there was already a huge fire inside. Later, the front wall was starting to buckle, and without warning, the Fourth Street side collapsed, forcing first responders (including Painesville Fire and Painesville Township Fire, which had been called to assist) to run for their lives.

The radiant heat from the fire was so bad, it caused exterior damage to nearby buildings, including one across the street.

HISTORIC CORNER: VINE AND ERIE STREETS

A.T. Hill & Company

Many important structures have stood on the corners of Erie and Vine Streets through the years, including a wooden frame store that was the first grocery store in Willoughby. It was built by John and Alice Lee Hill, who lived on Vine Street and built a row of two-story brick homes. They had three daughters, with only one surviving past infancy, Alice T. Hill.

The wooden store was replaced by a two-story brick building in 1915, which was run by Alice T. and John's nephew, Edward P. Walsh, after John's death, and called A.T. Hill & Company.

A.T. Hill & Co. sign. *Courtesy of Willoughby Historical Society.*

Years later, likely after the Willoughby Viaduct opened in 1921, the original wooden building was moved to Kirtland on Route 6, where it was called the Olde Towne Tavern.

The Andrews School for Girls

A written history in the Willoughby Historical Society archives says, "Dr. Card-Dr. Orson-St. John-Andrews home and grounds faced Erie Street, bounded by Third and Vine Streets." This was Margaret St. John's childhood home and that of her mother, Louise Card. Margaret married Wallace C. Andrews in 1867 and lived on Euclid Avenue in Cleveland, where Wallace was busy with his Standard Oil businesses. By 1877, they moved to the Card–St. John homestead on the southwest corner of Erie and Vine but moved to New York City a few years later. According to *Pioneer Families of Cleveland*, they lived in a big home in a fashionable part of the city, and in 1899, while the wife and three children of Margaret's brother Gamliel were visiting their home, a gas explosion ripped through the house, killing Mr. and Mrs. Andrews, Gamliel's wife and children and two servants.

CP&A in downtown Willoughby, in front of a fire at the Kingsley Hotel; original Andrews School is in back upper left corner. *Courtesy of Willoughby Historical Society.*

According to their wills, the Andrewses wanted money from their estate to be used to establish a school in Willoughby "for the free education of girls with a special view toward rendering them self-supporting." It was stated in the will that if a school couldn't be built, the money should go to the Smithsonian Institution.

After a decade-long court battle, Andrews School for Girls opened at the former mansion on Erie and Vine, becoming the school's first building. The building was later replaced by the old Willoughby Post Office. The current site of Andrews Osborne Academy, down the street on Mentor Avenue, was purchased in 1913, and the campus school buildings and dormitories were built.

Bakeries, Soda Fountains and Drugstores

The comforting smell inside a bakery brings back memories of home-baked delights; however, in the late 1800s and early 1900s, a mobile bakery delivered tasty treats through the streets of Fairport.

Fairport Bakery, in business from 1898 to 1926, brought home-baked bread and other bakery items directly to its customers. It is believed to be the first bakery with a truck in Lake County, and a photo shows that the side of the truck promoted its business telephone number as simply "5."

Hough Bakeries

Many are nostalgic for the tastes and smells of a visit to Hough Bakeries. It began on Hough Avenue in Cleveland in 1903, and through the early 1970s, it was the place to go to order specialty cakes and goodies. There were several Hough Bakeries locations throughout Lake County, including one in Painesville and two in Willoughby.

Jane Fosnot-Sweeney recalled on the Facebook page "Wonderful Willoughby, Ohio": "My family bought all of our bakery from Hough's in Downtown Willoughby."

Hough Bakeries was a special treat any time of the year but especially during holidays like Easter, when many remember enjoying a lamb- or bunny-shaped cake and petits fours for dessert. "If only you could eat your memories," said William Dorsey, in a comment on the "Wonderful Willoughby, Ohio" page.

Top: Hough Bakery in Painesville, circa early 1950s. *Courtesy of Mary Ann Podd Bukky.*

Bottom: 1965 *News-Herald* Hough Bakeries Easter ad. *Courtesy of Brad Sullivan.*

Marshall's Drug Company and Standard Drug Company

At one time, Marshall's Drug Company and Standard Drug Company were located diagonally across from each other in downtown Willoughby. (Standard was where Mularkey's Irish Pub currently is, and Marshall's was at the site of present-day Chagrin River Tavern.)

When Stephen Rae was a kid, he took music lessons at Fine Arts, when it was originally in the building that now houses the Homestead House B&B on West Spaulding.

In between our waiting for lessons, my sister [Barbara] and I would go to this counter and order hot toast with butter. We would put jelly on the toast from the small jelly packets. We loved our treat and sitting at the counter like grown-ups. My brother Michael would turn me on to the glazed donuts across the street at Hough Bakeries. I was in 10-year-old heaven in DTW.

Many also remember the warm, "square" hot dog buns and fountain Coke.

Debbie and James Lewis have a more than fifty-year love story that began at Marshall's Drug. Although she now lives in Tennessee, Debbie grew up in downtown Willoughby, in the apartments above the businesses, along with her extended family.

Woolworth's was down there. That was next to Marshall's. I used to go there all the time when I was little. It was really neat. You'd walk in, the fountains were on the right and the store area was on the left and the pharmacy was way in the back. It was the old-time counter with sodas and sandwiches and things like that and the same girls worked there for years and years.

When she was almost fifteen years old, a friend offered her tickets to go see Sonny and Cher on a blind date with his friend.

"I was supposed to meet them there at Marshall's at six o'clock, and they never showed up. I was really mad."

She knew her date's name was Jim Lewis. "I was talking to a lady who worked there, Vi, and said I'm going to call him and see what's going on. I went over to the phone, hanging on the wall, got the phone book and looked up Lewis."

Downtown Willoughby, circa late 1960s; Marshall's Drug is on the right and Cleveland Trust Bank on the left. *Photo by Marilyn Esposito.*

Left: Wilma Jean Hendrix working at Standard Drug in Downtown Willoughby, circa early 1950s. *Courtesy of Kim Hendrix Hurst.*

Right: "Soda jerk" working at Standard Drug in Downtown Willoughby, early 1950s. Chocolate sodas cost twenty cents. *Courtesy of Kim Hendrix Hurst.*

As it turned out, Jim thought he was supposed to go with another girl, but when he realized it was Debbie (whom he knew of through friends at South High School, where they were both students), he eagerly agreed to meet. "We just sat there at Marshall's at the counter, and he got me a drink, and we sat and talked for about three hours," recalls Debbie.

She went to a dance the following Saturday night at the courthouse with a group of girlfriends. "I told him we were going, and he was a greaser—he walks in with this black leather jacket on and his friends. He came over and picked me up off the floor and said, 'We've got to talk.' I was shocked."

They decided to start dating that night, got engaged a year later and got married in 1967, before Jim left after being drafted into the Vietnam War. They now have four kids, ten grandchildren and nine great-granddaughters, and it all began at Marshall's.

"It was home away from home. All the kids that I hung out with, we hung out at Marshall's drugstore. We never got in trouble, never caused any trouble. It was just our hangout."

In 1950, a large fire spread throughout Marshall's Drug Store, F.W. Woolworth and Pizzi Shoe Repair. It caused nearly $400,000 in damage and destroyed the buildings of Marshall's and Woolworth. Marshall's was later rebuilt.

The 1952 Marshall's Drug fire in downtown Willoughby. *Courtesy of Willoughby Historical Society.*

African American Business Trailblazers

Henry C. Dawson

In 1865, Captain Ransom Kennedy (who had a lakefront farm in present-day Willowick and was one of the first rescuers to reach the *G.P. Griffith* shipwreck) moved to Willoughby. Several years later, he opened a grocery store and tinshop (a shop where tinware was made or repaired), called R. Kennedy & Son with his eldest son, Hiram (one of seven children he and his wife, Laura White, had).

After Ransom Kennedy's death in 1887 (at fifty-six years old), the store continued as Kennedy and Rockafellow and later as Willoughby Hardware, which operated until the 1990s. (The stained-glass window with that name can still be seen from the sidewalk under the canopy in front of the building's current occupant, Fiona's Coffee Shop.)

A small building next door was split between two competing barbers: Henry C. Dawson and Felix Jones. According to an account written by local historian Frank Shankland decades ago, found in the historic archives of the Little Red Schoolhouse in Willoughby, Dawson (1844–1928) was "a highly respected colored man, the only representative of his race in town."

Dawson, who was just a teenager when the Civil War began, was ahead of his time in owning his own business, particularly in a White-dominated town. However, even before emancipation, free and enslaved African Americans were finding innovative ways to start their own businesses. From about 1900 to 1930, there was a "golden age" of Black-owned businesses in the United States. This was in part due to the Jim Crow laws that forced African Americans to form separate communities, which led to an entrepreneurship boom. Booker T. Washington founded the National Negro Business League in 1900, which helped grow Black-owned businesses.

When a fire ripped through downtown Willoughby in the early 1880s (the first of two major fires in two years), Dawson's barbershop suffered a loss of $350, a huge sum of money at the time, but he was a shrewd businessman and had insurance, according to an article from the November 9, 1883 *Independent*. Dawson and his wife, Kate, had a daughter named Anna. This local business pioneer is buried in the Willoughby Village Cemetery.

Roy H. Johnson

Roy H. Johnson was born in Painesville, where he also attended high school, and he later owned a barbershop in Fairport Harbor from the 1950s through at least the '70s.

Many residents, like Bruce E. Mackey, have fond memories of going to him for a cut. "He cut my hair many times," says Mackey, whose dad took him there routinely. "They were great, and I enjoyed going there."

Betty Silvi recalled, "He was my husband's barber. He gave my then-eighteen-month[-old] his first of many haircuts in his life. He was a very nice gentle quiet man."

Betty's baby, Lee Silvi, grew up to be Fairport Harbor fire chief and a well-respected local historian who shared with me this next bit of interesting information. According to *Hometown Sketches, 1796–1936*, Johnson was not known just as the local barber but also for his skills as a musician. The book reads, "He was the leader of Johnson's Orchestra, a jazz band, for many years and still takes an interest in music, playing several instruments."

Roy had a long lineage in Lake County. He was a relative of Harvey H. Johnson, born in 1828, believed to have been the first African American citizen of Lake County. He first came through the county as an escaped slave and eventually went to Canada, where African Americans were being offered land and money, and churches and schools were flourishing.

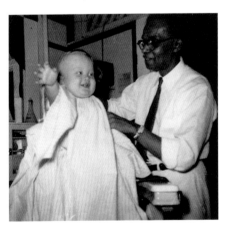

After the end of the Civil War, Johnson returned to Painesville and opened a barbershop on Railroad Street in Painesville. He died at the age of 101 and is buried in Ashtabula. His barbershop was passed on through the generations to his son James and then his grandson. His legacy lives on through his descendants, like Wendell P. Walker, who was president of the Painesville City Council.

Lee Silvi's first haircut by Fairport barber Roy H. Johnson. *Courtesy of Lee Silvi, photo by Betty Silvi.*

Dr. William and Mrs. Mildred Rucker

Dr. William Rucker was born in Nashville, Tennessee, in 1898, and while he was growing up, two events changed the course of his life, steering him into the field of medicine. When his arm swelled and became infected after he received a vaccination as a teen, a doctor at his church healed him. Later, his uncle died in a hospital from a ruptured appendix.

Both experiences had such a great impact on him that, after receiving a bachelor's degree from Fisk University, he decided to attend Meharry Medical College in Nashville, Tennessee, which was the first medical school for African Americans in the South. According to the Lake County branch of the NAACP, after earning his medical degree, he married his wife, Mildred L. Rucker, in 1927 and moved to Cleveland in 1929, opening a practice where he served for many years. Nearly a decade later, he and his wife settled in Painesville, which they heard about from Reverend Calvert, pastor of St. John Baptist Church.

When Dr. Rucker first arrived in Painesville, he applied to Lake Memorial Hospital as a staff doctor, but at the time, he wasn't even allowed to take the test to be considered for employment at the hospital because he was Black. However, when he applied again later and took the test, he had the third-highest score, and he was hired on at the hospital in the late 1930s.

Francee Vosicky Morse says he was "a very fine doctor and gentleman." Not only was Morse born at Lake County Memorial Hospital, but she also worked there as a registered nurse for forty-six years and worked with Dr. Rucker. "I admired Dr. Rucker for his gentle, caring ways, not only with his patients but with the staff as well," Morse says. "I never heard him raise his voice or berate a nurse, and he seemed to have great respect from fellow doctors."

According to the 1940 census, Dr. Rucker was forty-one at the time, and his wife, Mildred L. Rucker, was thirty-six. They lived on West Jackson Street in Painesville. By 1944, Dr. Rucker started a private practice based out of his house, and his wife acted as both a nurse and office manager for her husband.

"I knew them as Grandma and Grandpa Rucker," said Anita (Gorby) Alvarado. "I loved them very much. When I had to see him, I'd take my plastic Lassie dog. And he'd treat her, too. I miss them both."

Patricia Cassell remembers taking her son to see Dr. Rucker in his home office in the 1960s: "Great doctor, with compassion. My baby was sick, and he called a cab to take me to the hospital—in those days, women didn't drive."

"I remember, as a very young child, Dr. Rucker making house calls to my grandmother's house to care for me," recalled Janice Boone Lichtenberger.

Dr. William Rucker of Painesville. *Courtesy of Earnestine Jones.*

Mrs. Mildred Rucker of Painesville. *Courtesy of Earnestine Jones.*

Many Painesville residents recall that Dr. Rucker always had beautiful flower arrangements in his front window, because besides loving and caring for people, he also loved nature and grew flowers and other plants on his eight-acre property. He was also president of the Lake County Garden Club.

Dunbar "Danny" T. Watson Jr. lived on Jefferson Street, about a fifteen-minute walk from Dr. and Mrs. Rucker's house. Not only did Dr. Rucker deliver him in 1959, but Watson also remembers the doctor coming to his home when he was sick.

"Yes, he was a good man, but what I remember most of all was his shots!!!" He said one day, Dr. Rucker was seated up front as a guest at his church. "After service, I walked up to him (I must have been six or seven), stared him in the face, locked onto his eyes, and shouted from the bottom of my heart, 'YOUR SHOTS HURT!!!'"

Watson lived in Painesville until 1976, and although he'll always remember Dr. Rucker's kindness, he'll also never forget those shots.

Both Dr. and Mrs. Rucker became important contributors to Lake County. The Lake County branch of the NAACP, which they were instrumental in establishing, says the Ruckers were very involved at St. John Baptist Church, holding leadership roles and donating time and money. Dr. Rucker was a Sunday school teacher, a longtime deacon and a dynamic leader in the building of the new church.

"It was said that they 'literally touched the lives of every African American child born in Painesville,' during their time here," according to the Lake County History Center. "The Ruckers wanted to instill a belief in African-American children that they could do great things." They mentored them, teaching them self-respect, and took them on field trips to museums, amusement parks and gardens. "I remember as a girl she [Mrs. Rucker] had us girls from St. John's Baptist Church at her house and at the church for youth meetings," recalled Wanda Sowell-Council.

Dr. William and Mrs. Mildred Rucker of Painesville. *Courtesy of Earnestine Jones.*

According to the Lake County History Center, Mildred was also the first African American woman in Lake County's chapters of the American Red Cross, American Cancer Society and Lake County League of Women Voters. In 1972, she received an honorary PhD in liberal arts from Lake Erie College in recognition of her years of service at the college. Dr. Rucker is believed to have been the first and only African American doctor in Lake County for more than three decades.

Dr. William and Mildred Rucker dedicated their lives to giving back to the community, and their impact is still being felt today. In 2018, the Dr. William J. Rucker Community Medical Award was created through the Lake County NAACP.

Chapter 6
RESORTS AND LEISURE

V ibrant watercolor sunsets, the relaxing sound of the rolling waves and
the cool breeze drifting off the lake have been luring visitors to the
shores of Lake Erie for more than a century.

As nearby cities grew, hardworking industrialists were drawn to its calming
shores. Clevelanders enjoyed taking a break from their busy schedules and
the grit and smog of the city by traveling east via interurban trains and
even ferries, which were said to have sailed along the shoreline, stopping at
various parks.

MADISON TOWNSHIP PARK

On July 4, 1813, a community picnic was held at Phineas Mixer's cabin at the
shore, according to *Madison*, by Denise Michaud and the Madison Historical
Society. The Madison Harvest Festival later took place at Madison Township
Park in Madison-on-the-Lake. A 1907 photo shows visitors arriving to the
festival, parking their buggies near the pavilion, which provided shelter for
dances and parties. It was a popular destination until it burned down in 1933.

The forty-five-room Cottage Grove Inn, just east of Madison Township
Park, was built in 1914 by Judd W. Snell, who also operated the Park Hotel in
Madison Village from 1902 to 1915. It was a luxurious setting for vacationers,
with a shaded lawn overlooking Lake Erie. It was demolished in 1962, and
homes were built on the site.

Cottage Grove Inn, Madison on the Lake. *Courtesy of Madison Historical Society.*

MADISON GOLF LAKELANDS

Nearby, the Madison Golf Lakelands was started on Chapel Road in 1921. Fairways were leveled, irrigation pipes were added and a nine-hole golf course opened on Route 20 in 1925. From the '20s through '40s, club members had to own property in the course and pay a ten-dollar initiation fee, ten dollars in annual dues and one-dollar green fees.

The golf course and country club featured family entertainment, with a children's day camp, three dances a week, game night and weekly movies. It changed its name to Madison Country Club in the early 1960s.

Much of the lakeshore throughout Lake County was dotted with summer cottages, which were sold and rented to vacationers, in the late 1800s and early 1900s. The Boosters Club in Madison published a *Vacationer's Guide* in 1931, providing information for visitors, including train and bus schedules and entertainment options in the region.

PERRY TOWNSHIP PARK

Perry Township Park was another lakefront stop for visitors to enjoy the view of a sunset, listen to some music and dance in the pavilion, which was built

Beach at Perry Township Park. *Courtesy of Jack Kless/Perry Historical Society.*

Pavilion at Perry Township Park. *Courtesy of Jack Kless/Perry Historical Society.*

in 1908 with handmade bricks. Some recall music and dancing even into the 1960s and square dancers on Saturday nights, according to Mary Platko's *A Little Bit of Perry History*.

Back in those early days, there was a broad lawn with a sidewalk leading to steps going down toward a sandy beach. The old pavilion was dismantled over time by crashing waves, and the pieces the lake spared were removed in the 1970s.

Linden Beach

Heading west down the shore, in Painesville Township, Linden Beach was founded on the north end of Hardy Road, on what had been Governor Huntington's farm, in 1870. Visitors enjoyed its dining room and tent colonies for the next quarter century.

Just to the west of Linden Beach sat the two-story Shore Club, established in 1898 on the Lathrop and Smart farms (the site would later become Diamond Alkali). Visitors enjoyed the lake view from the porches of the green two-story Club House building or stayed in the nearby cottages through 1921.

Fairport Harbor Lakefront Park has been the site of summertime fun for more than a century. Years ago, the bandstand was a focal point at the park.

Mentor Beach Park

In 1891, the CP&E interurban railroad extended to Mentor, costing thirty-five cents a ticket to get to stop 58 at Center Street, which took one hour and thirty-five minutes. This brought even more people to the flourishing beach resorts in Mentor-on-the-Lake and Mentor Headlands.

Mentor Beach Park, located on Lakeshore Boulevard, in Mentor-on-the-Lake, was first established in 1899 as Mentor Township Park. From the 1930s to 1950s, it was connected to Mentor Beach Playland, a small amusement park that featured a dance hall (where the big bands of the era played), rides (including a wooden carousel), games and arcades. There was also a nearby roller-skating rink that opened around 1908, still operating today as Joy's Roller Rink.

Lola Carlton holding Orlo Carlton at Mentor Beach Park, circa 1920s. *Courtesy of Lynn Carlton.*

Skip Brolund grew up nearby in Grand River, where his parents, Gene and Karen Brolund, still live and remembers going to Walton's roller rink as a kid in the 1970s every Sunday night with his parents and siblings, Lisa and Scott. "We always had an early supper on Sundays then went skating and came home and usually had some kind of dessert and watched the typical Sunday night TV lineup, which if I remember correctly was probably Marlin Perkins's *Wild Kingdom*."

Skip's father worked at the roller arena in high school, so visiting it with his own children brought back happy memories. (As the story goes, he was also an excellent skater and considered touring with his skating partner but went into military service instead.)

Skip remembers an organ that played every weekend and was sad to see that it was gone when he visited several years ago. So he did some research and discovered these instruments are often tracked on enthusiast websites, which is where he found information on that organ.

In the April 2019 journal of the Carousel Organ Association of America, Skip discovered a Wurlitzer Band organ—a type of organ installed in theaters and carousels in the early twentieth century because it could project music loudly enough to be heard above the din—had spent time at the Mentor Playland skating rink.

The Wurlitzer Band organ number 3437 was first shipped to St. Louis, Missouri, in 1922, and by 1925, it was rebuilt and entertaining visitors to

Coney Island amusement park in Cincinnati. In 1953, it was rebuilt into a 165 style, and its last public home was at the Mentor-on-the-Lake roller-skating rink. A one-foot strip was cut from the middle of the facade's top crest to clear the ceiling, and it was painted an off-white with pink and baby blue accents.

Every night, at closing time, owner Howard Walton played roll number 6510, "Home Sweet Home," a medley of four waltzes, to notify patrons that it was time to leave, including: "Good Night Ladies," "We Won't Go Home Till Morning," "Auld Lang Syne" and "Then We'll Go Home." The organ eventually made its way to a Rhode Island collector and has been passed down in his family.

As an interesting side note, Skip's family played a role in naming his hometown. "My father's father, who was also legally named Eugene Alfred Brolund, just as my father and myself, lived in Grand River, Ohio, and at one time was a Lake County sheriff, township trustee, thirty-second-degree mason and, among other things, port authority and mayor of Grand River." During his term as mayor, he changed the name from Richmond to Grand River, "due to the fact that there were several other Richmond, Ohios, and this was before the days of zip codes, so mail was constantly going to the wrong places."

He says that's why Richmond Road is in Painesville and Painesville Township, because it was Richmond, Ohio, at one point.

Salida Beach

Salida Beach, on Lake Drive, was also a popular vacation spot at the turn of the century. According to an advertisement in the *Painesville Republican*, it was near the Nickel Plate railway and the CP&E trolley line.

"Everything is first class, best service, boating, fishing, hunting, and bathing. Special attention to private parties; elegant cottages when desired. Free telephone connection at Mentor, O. is provided." The advertisement continues to say that the cottages and three-story resort hotel, known for its wide porches, are open from June 1 to October 31.

The hotel was later bought by the Ohio Episcopal Diocese for use by the Girls' Friendly Society (to encourage purity of life, dutifulness to parents, faithfulness to employers and thrift) as a "Holiday House." A 1908 *Church Life* newsletter says the diocesan and branch officers felt the need of a place

THE GIRL'S FRIENDLY SOCIETY HOLIDAY HOUSE AT SALIDA BEACH, MENTOR, OHIO.

Postcard of the Girl's Friendly Society Holiday House at Salida Beach, Mentor. *Author's collection.*

We always meet at

Willoughby, O.

Let's meet again

Postcard promoting Willoughby, Ohio, as a tourist destination. *Courtesy of Rachel Vanek, from the collection of Joseph and Betty Koelliker Jr.*

where their girls could go at a moderate expense for rest and recreation during summer vacations. Such Holiday Houses were owned and well patronized in Michigan, Pennsylvania, New York and other states.

The newsletter goes on to state that the Salida Beach property was offered to the society the previous year: "Two and a half acres of timbered land, having a supply of natural spring water, good drainage, rights to the use of 225 feet of lake front for bathing, a living room, dining room, etc. and furniture; a cottage of six rooms, and an ice house."

Lisa Layton, who worked for the Mentor Public Library for more than twenty years, created the Mentor-on-the-Lake History Buffs group to allow library patrons to gather at the Mentor-on-the-Lake branch, share their memories and reminisce about the area's early days. They particularly enjoy talking about Mentor Beach Playland and the Salida Hotel and dance hall.

"One man told me he was a drummer who filled in at the dance hall there," Layton recalled. "He said that Lana Turner took him by the hand and led him onto the stage. His eyes lit up when he told the story. He took me back there."

Will-O-Bee on the Lake/North Willoughby

In the early 1900s, the north end of Willoughby was a summer resort community called Will-O-Bee, also spelled "Willobee-on-the-Lake," dotted with summer cottages, beckoning visitors from afar.

A 1919 promotional brochure asks:

> *Had your vacation yet? For less than you would spend on that trip you've planned you may make a substantial payment on a lot and cottage at Willobee-on-the-Lake, the ideal summer cottage allotment for discriminating people. We are prepared to build your cottage to suit your ideas, on your lot in a week to 10-days. The terms are easy on both lots and cottages. At Will-O-Bee on the Lake vacation pleasures may be yours all summer, every summer.*

The Willobee Shore Club was on Beachview Road, at the end of Lost Nation Boulevard, where Sunset Park is now. According to a postcard, the community club had buffet service, a dance floor, a beach stairway and a bathing pier; the postcard called it Cleveland's newest "Summer Happiness" colony.

Many remember the "old Swiss house," in the nearby North Willoughby neighborhood, at 111 Cherokee Trail. Local historian Bill Barrow, retired head of special collections in the Michael Schwartz Library at Cleveland State University/Cleveland Memory project, recalls living at the Swisscott home with his family from 1952 to 1962. "It was a great place for a kid to grow up in," he remembers fondly. "Lots of fantasy material."

According to Barrow, the huge house, towering over the one-story homes on Cherokee Trail for six to seven decades, was named for its builders, the Scott family. "I was surprised in recent years to learn that building Swiss chalet–type homes, though not on this scale necessarily, in modest lakefront neighborhoods wasn't uncommon," explained Barrow.

He remembers the house had two front doors, a porch across the front and a first floor with a large living room and big stone fireplace. The third floor had a master bedroom and bathroom and four small bedrooms around a balcony looking down into the living room.

The house burned down in the 1990s, and not a trace is left in the redevelopment of its large yard with two new homes.

Barrow has lived in several other historic homes, including one of four houses built to be part of a Spanish Colonial subdivision on Granada Drive promoted as "Venice on Lake Erie." The plans for the subdivision never moved forward when the Great Depression began; however, Mentor Harbor Yacht Club was created at the site of the main building, built in the popular Spanish-style architecture of the time, overlooking the lake.

Barrow also lived at an 1825 Greek/Federal Revival house on the southwest corner of Chillicothe Road and Mentor Avenue, built by Jonathan Goldsmith, renowned Western Reserve master builder, for Joseph Sawyer.

Chagrin Harbor Beach

"Near the joining of the Chagrin River and Lake Erie, Chagrin Harbor Beach was settled first as a summer week-end community where, on Sunday nights, the families headed back for the city," states an old newspaper clipping (with the date and newspaper name omitted) found at the Eastlake Historical Society (in Eastlake City Hall). The article explains that the wartime housing shortage caused some families to remodel cottages into year-round homes, and soon other weekenders decided not to head back to the city.

Grandchildren of Frank and Helen Beerer, of Wicklow Drive, at the beach in Eastlake, circa 1944/1945. *Courtesy of Eastlake Historical Society.*

As a permanent settlement, the Eastlake community has retained its fondness for family fun. For mom, there are the household chores to be done, but if she steps along, there's still time for an afternoon swim with the youngsters.

Pop willingly drives the 22 miles if he works downtown because he knows that can of worms he dug the night before is waiting and, if he feels real lazy, he can toss his line in from his or the neighbor's backyard.

And for the youngsters—well, in this Lake County community, parents seldom hear that sad vacation-time lament: "Mom, I don't have nothin' to do."

WILLOUGHBEACH

On the far western end of the county, Willoughbeach Park, in present-day Willowick, was perhaps the most famous Lake County beach resort of its day. Opening in 1898, it was situated on the lakeshore, across parts of Cresthaven Drive, Lakeshore Boulevard, Sylvan Drive and Bruce Lane. It began with cottages, dance pavilions and bathing areas and transformed into an amusement park with rides and a car coaster, named the Jack Rabbit. It was created by CP&E owners Edward Moore and Henry Everett and conveniently had an interurban stop right in front (which allowed them to profit from visitors traveling to the site and enjoying the park). It was also a

Postcard of smiling couple at Willoughbeach Amusement Park. *Author's collection.*

Postcard of American Clay Company employee picnic at Willoughbeach, in front of baseball stands. *Author's collection.*

popular spot for company picnics, and most of the postcards available from the park are from the American Clay Machinery Company picnic in 1913.

Willowick Country Club

Across the street from where Willoughbeach once stood is Shoregate Shopping Center, which has transitioned over the years from a grand strip mall, one of the first of its kind in Lake County, to one about half its original size.

The shopping center used to contain shops and restaurants like the Fireplace Restaurant, the Ground Round and Faroh's Candies, which I have fond memories of visiting with my family as a kid. According to a summer 1992 *Shoregate Sentinel* newsletter, some of the stores at Shoregate in 1955 included Marshall Drug Company, Garfinkel Shoes, Kaase Bake Shops, Fisher Foods and Shoregate Hardware. By 1992, they included Fashion Bug (where I remember shopping with my mom), Lerner, Hair Care Harmony (many of the stylists are now at Marino's Hair Design in Willoughby), Record Shop and Medic Drug.

However, before the land was the site of an extensive shopping center, it was designed to be a golf course with neatly manicured green grass, rolling hills and steep gullies. On August 28, 1910, a *Plain Dealer* article announced: "Plans have been completed for the formation of the Willowwick Country club, on the lake shore just east of Willoughbeach and an application has been filed for incorporation papers for the company."

Moore, who co-owned the CP&E interurban railway and Willoughbeach Amusement Park, was also one of the founders of the golf course, which drew even more visitors to his already popular rail line stop. Clevelanders came in by the hundreds for company picnics at Willoughbeach, and now they would have another leisure escape.

According to a headline in the September 18, 1910 *Plain Dealer:* "Work on New Willowick Clubhouse to be started within ten days. Golf expert to be engaged to lay out eighteen-hole course." The directors named for the new organization included Ralph L. Fuller, E.V. Hale (who, according to a 1915 map, owned land along the lake east of Willoughbeach), Charles A. Otis, Edward W. Moore, A.G. Clark, Henry Dreher, G.B. Durell (who owned land east of Willoughbeach next to E.V. Hale) and E. VanGorder.

Many of these men were business moguls of their day, including Charles Otis, who owned a large portion of Waite Hill and was involved in the iron,

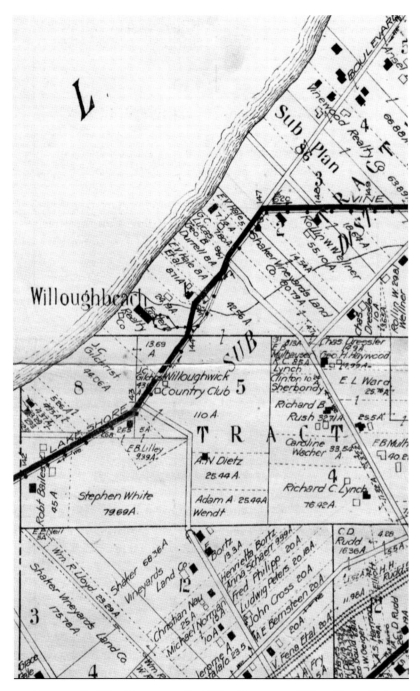

A 1915 map of Willoughby, present-day Willowick, showing Willoughbeach Park and Willoughwick Country Club. *Courtesy of Lakecountyohio.gov.*

steel, telephone and Cleveland newspaper industries. He was also one of the original members of the Kirtland Country Club, along with Moore, which originally had been built as the home of his business partner Henry Everett, so the lives of these businessmen were intertwined at several other luxury sites in northeast Ohio, and Willowick Country Club was their next venture.

"It will front directly on Lake Erie, with about eight acres devoted to club grounds, tennis courts and other amusement features," states the September 18, 1910 article. "The golf [course] will lie south of the road, which is now being improved with a brick pavement. A prominent local architect is to be formally engaged within a day or two to proceed with plans for the club house and outbuildings, including a large garage for the automobile features of the new club, which will be important."

A survey plat was drawn up the same year by F.A. Pease Engineering Company of Cleveland, showing the golf course located within the borders of Lake Shore Boulevard to the north, Rush Road (now East 305th Street) to the east and Worden Road (East 293rd Street) to the west, on land that had been farmlands and vineyards.

The *Plain Dealer* explains that groundbreaking ceremonies would be held soon so the clubhouse would be ready by the following summer. And with paved roads leading to the new club from all directions, a colony of bungalows was to be built up near the golf links, for club members.

Besides golfing, the new club was planning to offer yachting, boating, canoeing, tennis and trap shooting. "A liberal number of sleeping rooms will be provided in the club house to accommodate members who desire to go there and pass the weekend or enjoy a few days outing in the country."

Less than a year later, it was apparent that the golf club founders had decided to remodel the former farmhouse of Ransom Kennedy, already located on the site, to use as a temporary clubhouse.

An April 23, 1911 *Plain Dealer* article says:

The structure is in a first-class state of preservation and the alterations and changes will provide a comfortable and convenient housing for the club in the next year, even if it is a little smaller than the new structure will be when completed. The old barn is being arranged for garage purposes and will easily be made ready for use. The one additional and exceptionally pleasing feature of the location of the club's site lies in the fact that the interurban cars run very near while the roads out from the city are always in first class condition. So travel by car or auto is always fast.

Willowick Country Club clubhouse, 1924. *Courtesy of City of Willowick.*

The article explains that the links, when completed, would be about 6,200 yards in length, "sufficient to give the long players every chance and at the same time leaving enough short holes to properly balance the whole course." Hole 13 would be the longest, at 568 yards.

The double *w* spelling of "Willowwick Country Club" earlier in this story was not a typo—it was possibly the earliest printing of a name that would later encompass an entire city (Willowick would become an official city in 1957).

The April 23, 1911 *Plain Dealer* article continues,

> *The name is singularly euphonious and is derived from the location of the tract the club purchased between Willoughbeach and Wickliffe. At the outset the land was particularly well adapted for a golf course.... There are natural bunkers that will make the links much more sporty than ordinary farms would produce.*

Several years later, the name is written in a 1915 Lake County atlas as "Willoughwick Country Club," so perhaps the early founders had varying opinions of how the country club's name should be spelled.

The club started out with nine holes, but the eighteen-hole course was completed in May 1913 under the direction of golf course aficionado Jack Way. (He was also involved in creating and conditioning Canterbury Golf Club in Cleveland, where he was known as "Mr. Everything" from the 1920s to early '40s.)

Gale Lippucci, longtime library associate of adult services at Willowick Public Library, compiled the fascinating "Willowick History Project" on the library's site, which describes Willowick as a private course, par seventy, with eighteen holes spanning 154 acres. According to the site,

> Eight of those acres were on the north side of the boulevard and included the clubhouse. A tunnel ran under Lake Shore Boulevard connecting the course to the clubhouse. The golf course was known for its many sand traps. The most difficult hole was no. 6, which was cut by a deep gully and was known as the "canyon" hole.

In his research on Willowick Country Club, Willowick mayor Rich Regovich discovered a 1915 printed booklet brochure titled *The Fair Sex Are Welcome at Willowick*. The front cover shows female golfers and a photo of male and female golfers, saying, "Punch Bowl Hole No. 9 at Willowick Country Golf Club." The back cover shows drawings of male golfers and a full-length photo of Jack Way posing with a golf club. This is evidence that, in this aspect, the club was ahead of its time by welcoming women in a male-dominated sport.

In fact, Lippucci and her coworker Lora Scibelli did some research after receiving a request for information from a woman who works at an antique shop in Michigan who came across a silver trophy etched with "Humphrey Trophy, Willowick Country Club, Ladies September Flight, 1917, won by Mrs. John P. Franck."

Through research, they discovered that Harriet and John Franck seemed to move quite often and had lived in affluent neighborhoods in Cleveland and Willoughby Township. The Cleveland Blue Books of 1922 and 1924 listed John P. Franck as a member of the country club (along with Henry Everette, Penfield as first vice president and Feargus B. Squire as the secretary).

The Humphrey Tournament was likely sponsored by the Humphrey family, who owned and operated Euclid Beach Park in Cleveland, since

Hole no. 6 gully at Willowick Country Club. *Courtesy of Cleveland Memory Project, Cleveland State University.*

they would have had the financial means. Semiprofessional and amateur competitions were common among clubs in the 1910s and 1920s, but Harriet must have been a skilled golfer to participate and win.

While reading Rick Porello's book *Bombs, Bullets, & Bribes: The True Story of Notorious Jewish Mobster Alex Shondor Birns*, Regovich came across a surprising mention of the Willowick Country Club. Twenty-year-old mobster Alex Shondor Birns already had several arrests and a prison stretch to his name (at one point, he was labeled the city of Cleveland's "public enemy number one") when he connected with established gangsters in the area. He became the protégé of Maxie Diamond and his partner, Philip Goldberg, Woodland East Fifty-Fifth Street gang leaders affiliated with the Mayfield Road mob.

According to *Bombs, Bullets, & Bribes*, "Shondor became a frequent companion of Maxie Diamond, who was active in labor racketeering and operated nightclubs. Diamond managed the Willowick Country Club in Lake County just outside Cleveland. Birns partnered with him in another joint downtown, the Parisian Village Café."

According to Porrello's book, many foolish girls were enamored by the ways of the racketeer. "Runaway Clementina Damiano, thirteen, was a fan of *Little Caesar*, *Public Enemy*, and other mob movies. In the summer of 1933, she left New York City on a train bound for Chicago to fulfill her dream of becoming a gangster's sweetheart."

During a stopover in Cleveland, the police picked her up, and a probation officer tried to get her back home. The probation department didn't have the budget to buy her train fare, so the officer asked his fellow city employees for donations, but no one donated, so he came up with another idea.

> *If the girl was a fan of cinematic gangsters, maybe she would elicit sympathy from real gangsters. He headed up to the Willowick Country Club, a known mob hangout. Indeed, he found Tony Milano, Maxie Diamond, and his young associate Shondor Birns. When the men were told of the girl's plight, they didn't hesitate and reached deep. A few hours later the wannabe moll was riding a train back to New York City.*

At this point, Willowick Country Club was a public course, and the private members had moved to Manakiki Country Club (presently Manakiki Golf Course) on S.O.M. Center Road, in Willoughby, which had a grand opening the evening of May 6, 1930. A *News-Herald* article from that day says, "Dancing and cards will be a feature of the event, and a buffet supper will be served at ten o'clock."

The new clubhouse was transformed from the former estate of Howard M. Hanna (a well-known Cleveland businessman) on the Sleepy Hollow Farm, and the club already had many local members, including township trustee and businessman Conrad Albracht and his wife. Between six and seven hundred guests attended the formal event.

According to Lippucci, the Depression of the early 1930s and gas rationing during World War II took their toll on Willowick Country Club, and it was turned back into a nine-hole course and eventually closed in the 1950s. Today, the names of the streets are the only remnants left to remind residents of what the land used to be, including Fairway Boulevard, Bunker Road, Green Drive, High Tee Drive and Divot Drive.

THE TUNNEL

"The tunnel," as it was known, was originally built under Lakeshore Boulevard to connect golfers on the south side of the road with the clubhouse and course on the north side. (It crossed over approximately where the Giant Eagle Get Go gas station is today.)

In a 1998 *News-Herald* article, caddies recalled working at the golf course decades earlier. "Sometimes we had to carry their [the golfers'] bags through the tunnel clear to the parking lot," said Jim Marsh, who caddied at the course in the 1920s. "[The tunnel] was for members only." When the golf course went public in 1928, the clubhouse, along with the tunnel, became an entertainment hot spot, hosting big-name bands like Sammy Kay.

After the course closed, the multistory clubhouse became a temporary home for the Willowick public library, and pedestrians regularly used the tunnel to cross below the busy highway. Some people were scared to walk through—fearing who, or what, might be lurking inside—while others have fond memories.

Rosemary Macillas grew up near the end of East 305th Street, in Willowick, in the 1950s and '70s. She remembers seeing construction workers put up huge girders on the Federal's Department Store (where my dad has told me stories of getting his first bike) that was being built at Shoregate Shopping Center on the site of the old golf course and recalls regularly using the old tunnel.

> *It was so creepy, especially when cars went over the manholes and it would echo in the tunnel. I used to ride my bike as fast as I could to get through it. My mom took me there in a wagon when I was a toddler, and we would come home with a pile of books. I've loved libraries ever since.*

"I think I brought the whole series of Nancy Drew mysteries through that tunnel, three at a time," says Nancy Cozby, who lived on 324th Street. She said those books later inspired her to make her first car purchase, "a snappy little roadster." (Cozby's father, William, helped build Dudley Park.)

Sharon O'Flaherty, who served on the city council for two terms, grew up in Willowick as one of seven kids raised by her widowed mother. "I loved walking to the old library with my mom," O'Flaherty remembers. "The tunnel made it a great adventure."

In late August 1957, the threat of an explosion in the tunnel from an accumulation of gas forced the Willowick Library to close for at least a week.

Tunnel under Lake Shore Boulevard that linked the Willowick County Club clubhouse to the golf course in 1912. *Courtesy of Willowick Public Library and City of Willowick.*

East Ohio Gas Company crewmen discovered the leak when they were working on a nearby main line. The head librarian of the Willoughby-Eastlake district said the gas had seeped into the underground tunnel from the abandoned and deteriorating gas well seven hundred feet under the tunnel.

Hundreds of library patrons were disappointed when they arrived at the entrance to the tunnel to see it boarded up with a sign saying: "Stay Out—Danger—Gas Leak—No Smoking." During this time, librarian Janeth Shrewmaker got creative when she issued a plea for someone to lend the library a truck trailer to use as a temporary library to park in Shoregate Shopping Center for several days.

The passageway that had provided a memorable route to the library for so many was eventually shut down, plugged on both ends when Shoregate Shopping Center was constructed but left hollow in the middle.

In 1963, the Willowick Library moved to the new building on East 305th Street, and the old Willowick Golf Course clubhouse sat vacant, becoming a target of vandalism. Two years later, it was razed.

In the summer of 1998, road workers rediscovered the eight-by-eight-foot tunnel under Lakeshore Boulevard, about one thousand yards west of East 305th Street. In order to prevent a possible collapse, since only about a foot of concrete and steel separated the roadway from the tunnel, the Ohio Department of Transportation decided to fill the chamber with 220 cubic yards of low-strength mortar.

Filling in the passageway buried years of memories for many residents, but although it's no longer a tunnel, it remains a hidden link connecting us to Willowick's earliest days as a resort community.

LITTLE MOUNTAIN RESORT

Little Mountain Road runs through Mentor, Kirtland Hills and Concord Township, past some of the area's most historic buildings, like Wildwood and Hilo Farm. It's a reminder of the region's past, when it was a highly sought-after vacation destination for nearly one hundred summers.

From the early 1800s to early 1900s, the well-to-do ascended the mountain to relax and enjoy fresh air away from the noise and grittiness of downtown Cleveland, where many of them lived and worked. They longed for the unique beauty of this region, known as the "Saratoga Springs of the West" during its prime.

Little Mountain is unique geologically, a sandstone "sugarloaf" with an elevation of 1,266 feet. The *L*-shaped hill, capped by three knobs that line up at present-day Holden Arboretum, spans the border of Lake and Geauga Counties and peaks at Lake County's highest point, Daniels Mountain.

Little Mountain is a defined hill that was shaped by the forces of nature, with two ancient river systems that eroded land on either side: the Grand River to the east and Cuyahoga-Chagrin to the west, which flowed into a major river that predated Lake Erie. Because of its sharp rise in elevation and the winds coming in from Lake Erie, it has a distinctive climate that is cool in the summer and heavy with snow in the winter.

During its heyday, four hotels were built on the plateau, along with many cottages, which could accommodate hundreds of guests at a time, including well-known visitors like President James A. Garfield, John D. Rockefeller

143

and William H. Taft. Most of the buildings were built on the western side of the ridge, facing the cool breeze of Lake Erie and sweeping panoramic views, like the largest hotel, the Lake View House.

The start of Little Mountain's resort age began when Captain Simeon Reynolds settled in the area in the winter of 1817. By 1831, he had built the Little Mountain House hotel on seventy-five acres of land, with a road that led to the top, in hopes of turning the area into a resort destination. The hotel was spacious, with a bowling alley and observation platform to watch boats out on Lake Erie. Reynolds was said to enjoy playing his fiddle for dances held at his hotel.

Over the following decades, the hotel changed owners several times. Simeon sold it to his son, John Reynolds, who later sold it to Charles Avery. Under Avery's ownership and improvements, it was renamed Lake View House and could accommodate up to three hundred guests at a time.

According to Lake House advertisements, Little Mountain had a "dry atmosphere, cool nights, spring water, and the absence of mosquitoes, gnats, and flies."

The Stocking House, built by D.W. Stocking of Chardon, was the second hotel built on the summit, in 1850, and could house up to two hundred guests. It had a three-story main section, with two wings, a large observatory and a ballroom said to be the largest in northern Ohio. (Several decades later, in 1872, the Little Mountain Club bought the property and used the hotel as its clubhouse for over sixty years. In the 1940s, it was the last Little Mountain hotel to be demolished.)

In 1855, Drs. Rosa and Gatchell came up with the "water cure," offering resort-goers spring water they believed had healing properties. They purchased twenty-two acres of land south of the Lake View House and bargained with owner E.J. Ferris for use of a piece of his land and spring, adjoining their land on the west side of the mountain. William S. Gardiner became a partner in 1855, on the condition that he would build a boardinghouse, and it officially opened that year. The following winter, Rosa died, and Gatchell ran their business until 1857, when he sold it to Dr. Bagley of Chardon. Gatchell's partner, Gardiner, liquidated the company in 1857 but later completed the hotel that was originally supposed to be part of the water cure, the Little Mountain Eagle, which was three stories with two wings and an observatory on top.

The Little Mountain Eagle fell into ruin after Gardiner sold it in 1873 and nearly two decades later was torn down. Parts of the hotel were used to build the Church of the Transfiguration, which now stands as part of St. Hubert's.

Ad for the Little Mountain Eagle resort. *Courtesy of Concord Township/Stone Schoolhouse Museum.*

In 1891, Charles Avery tore down the Lake View House, which was not making a profit, and built the famed Pine Crest, a three-story building, shaped like a *T*, with a circular drive-up front.

The Pine Crest Hotel, surrounded by a fourteen-foot veranda, was the last hotel built on Little Mountain in the late 1880s and known as the most grand and elegant. An 1890 summer season brochure reads:

Guests standing in front of the Pine Crest Hotel on Little Mountain in Concord Township. *Courtesy of Concord Township/Stone Schoolhouse Museum.*

> *The guests' chambers are of good size and perfectly ventilated. They are single and en suite, with baths attached, private balconies, open fireplaces, etc. All principal rooms have ample clothes closets. Lavatories and hot and cold baths are on each floor. All rooms are connected with the office by an electronic call bell system. All rooms are lighted with gas. A baggage elevator as well as servant's staircase runs from basement to attic.*

The brochure goes on to highlight many other hotel features, including a Western Union telegraph office and post and express offices in the rotunda and entertainment for guests, like music played by an orchestra, billiards, bowling alleys and a maintained livery. (It was torn down around 1925, and stone from its foundation was used in the reconstruction of Shadybrook, summer home estate of the Arthur D. Baldwin family and former home of the Lake County History Center.)

The summer resort of Little Mountain was not only a playground for the rich, but it also became a source of income for local farmers, who provided produce and services to hotel guests. At the corner of Little Mountain and Morley Roads, a small village developed, known as Joice's Corners. A log schoolhouse was built in 1822, with Joseph Reynolds as the first teacher, and the last one-room schoolhouse in the area was built with red brick in 1885, at the corner of Little Mountain and King Memorial.

The rise of the automobile brought an end to Little Mountain, as visitors' travel options expanded. Gradually, the cottages and hotels were demolished, replaced by summer homes. In 1872, millionaire Randall P. Wade and a friend decided to create a private club. The Stocking House was bought, remodeled and renamed the Little Mountain Club, which had prominent members, including John D. Rockefeller and James A. Garfield. Some members bought farms and property near Little Mountain, but eventually membership declined, the club shares were sold, and it was torn down in 1941. As club members sold their shares, Ralph T. King bought their property, until the Kings owned most of the land on Little Mountain.

Today, the Holden Arboretum owns a small portion of the land that was originally the Little Mountain resort, but most of the remnants, including parts of old building foundations, remain on private property. Bottles have been found during unauthorized excavations around the hotel sites, since recycling didn't exist back then. In fact, the police are said to have quite a collection of confiscated materials that trespassers have uncovered.

Although Little Mountain's beauty certainly held an allure for visitors, as the region still does today, it also holds great scientific interest. Famous botanist John Riddell visited the area in 1836, from southern Ohio, to annotate the Western Reserve.

There are plants on the property dating back to Little Mountain's resort age and beyond. Brian Parsons, retired chief planning officer of Holden Arboretum, says that the Little Mountain area has been home to plants that don't exist anywhere else in Ohio, like the bristly sarsaparilla, which is a flowering perennial that was used for medicinal purposes. It was discovered in the Little Mountain area by Judy Bradt-Barnhardt while she was working on her college thesis in the 1980s, but it's unknown if it can still be found on-site today.

There are interesting sandstone caves on the property and old-growth hemlock and white pine trees that are hundreds of years old; some even predate European settlement. During the resort age, the trees were part of the mystique; resort owners cut down other trees and plants to allow the hemlocks and white pines to stand out.

Since 1971, several Little Mountain land parcels have been donated to the arboretum, which now owns 175 acres on and around Little Mountain and sometimes offers guided hikes to the area.

THE CHURCH OF THE TRANSFIGURATION

St. Hubert's Episcopal Church, on Baldwin Road in Kirtland Hills, is not only one of the oldest churches in Lake County but also the only surviving building that once stood atop Little Mountain in its resort days.

St. Hubert's, then named the Church of the Transfiguration, was built on the grounds of the Little Mountain Club in 1893. When the club declined and social activities came to an end, the Church of the Transfiguration stood vacant until 1916, when Bishop Leonard moved it seven miles to the Holiday House property at Salida Beach.

When it closed again in 1925, services were temporarily held on the front porch of Hollycroft in Mentor, the home of Helen and James R. Garfield, son of President James A. Garfield.

Four years later, the chapel was moved by horse and wagon to its present location on the bank of the Chagrin River East Branch in Kirtland Hills. It was renamed St. Hubert's, after the patron saint of hunters. Surprisingly, the beautiful stained-glass windows, made in Munich, Germany, and given as a gift to the church from members of the Little Mountain Club, survived the move, along with the bell and main framework.

The church initially operated as a summer chapel for four months a year. Years later, in 1970, year-round services began and continue today.

DANIEL CARTER BEARD

Although Daniel Carter Beard was born in Cincinnati in 1850, he moved to his grandparents' hometown of Painesville when he was young, where he enjoyed exploring the Little Mountain region and shores of Lake Erie. In Lake County, he learned how to hunt and fish and developed a love and respect for nature. In later years, after moving from Painesville, Beard became connected with many prominent people, including Mark Twain, whose books he illustrated; Theodore Roosevelt, who became a close friend; and Robert Baden-Powell, who started Scouts in England.

When Beard became editor of *Recreation*, he began the Society of the Sons of Daniel Boone for the young readers of the magazine, and with the help of Roosevelt, he eventually formed the Boy Scouts of America.

According to *Here Is Ohio's Lake County*, "Dan Beard has stated that 'he credits Painesville and Lake County's woods and streams for the vision he had as an adult of a new kind of recreation for boys, and out of this came American scouting."

Beard also came up with an idea to Americanize the Boy Scouts' fleur-de-lis by adding the American eagle and shield in 1911. He was granted the Roosevelt Distinguished Service Medal and was the U.S. national Scout commissioner from 1910 until his death in 1941.

Chapter 7

FILM, THEATER AND ENTERTAINMENT

THE PERILS OF SOCIETY

Cleveland industrialist and Waite Hill property owner Charles Otis was known for entertaining friends at his Pine Tree Farm. One of the great entertainments held at the farm was filming a movie called *The Perils of Society*, along with the luncheon Otis hosted for the cast, which included many Cleveland socialites.

The Perils of Society program. *From* Here I Am, *by Charles Otis.*

"I impersonated the country Squire and the company visited the farm several times," according to Otis's book *Here I Am*. "The theme of the story was the English polo team, had come over here to defeat the American team."

The game took place at the Hunt Club and various other Cleveland clubs. The group making the movie included Amasa Mather—son of Samuel Mather, who helped form Pickands, Mather & Company, which once had the largest shipping fleet on the Great Lakes—who was one of the players on the American team. At one point, the film ran out while filming an exhibition game, and the scene had to be filmed again, but the second time around,

Dinner with cast and crew of *The Perils of Society* with Charles Otis at his Pine Tree Farm in Waite Hill. *From* Here I Am, *by Charles Otis.*

Mather's horse fell over, and he was thrown to the ground, sustaining a "wrenched back."

The film was shown at the Metropolitan Theater on Euclid Avenue, near East 55th Street, and ran for two weeks. Proceeds of $11,000 from the film were donated to help with Belgian relief in 1915, during World War I.

ONE POTATO, TWO POTATO

In the summer of 1963, parts of Painesville were used as film locations for the movie *One Potato, Two Potato*. The drama was released in 1964 and centered on the story of a White woman (played by Barbara Barrie) who marries a Black man (Bernie Hamilton) and deals with issues surrounding the prejudices of the time.

According to Mark Meszoros's 2009 *News-Herald* article, when the movie was scheduled to be shown on the cable network Turner Classic Movies, it wasn't just locals who were looking forward to seeing it but also the Hollywood folks involved in the filming.

"All of us are looking forward to the 20th of this month," said Andrew Laszlo, the movie's director of photography and a veteran filmmaker. "We're all gearing up to make copies on VHS and DVD, what have you. No one seems to know who owns (the movie) or how to get a copy." Laszlo, whose cinematography credits included the first Rambo movie, *First Blood*, and *Star Trek V: The Final Frontier*, spent time searching the Internet for a copy. That's how he got to know Ron Gardner of Mentor.

Gardner says he became "the movie's official-unofficial local expert" after posting a review of the movie on the *New York Times* website, mentioning that he had a copy. His late grandfather Carl Gardner was one of many area residents who acted as an extra in the film and can be seen on the courthouse steps at the end of the movie. According to Gardner, "He was always a ham. He went down [to the filming], and the rest is history."

The movie was filmed at a downtown hotel, movie theater and park, the setting for a scene with a kiss between the two stars, which Richard Krown, the film's postproduction supervisor, said was the first interracial kiss of its kind on screen.

In the *News-Herald* article, cinematographer Laszlo said he thought the movie was filmed in and around Painesville because of director Larry Peerce's familiarity with northeast Ohio. But Krown believes it was producer Sam Weston's history with the area that brought the production there. Regardless, both men remember a very receptive town full of very friendly folks.

Laszlo recalls scenes taking place at a farmhouse outside of town. Krown remembers actor Robert Earl Jones, the father of James Earl Jones, eating a lot of corn right off the stalks in the farmer's field. "When we left, [the owner] said, 'You're going to have to pay me for all the corn that guy ate,'" Krown recalled.

Drive-Ins

There's something a bit magical about a drive-in movie: the stars above, the screen in front with a story unfolding, and all the while staying in the comfort of your own car.

Drive-in theaters were once a booming industry in Lake County, from the 1940s through the 1980s, with five locations in North Madison, Concord Township, Mentor, Eastlake and Wickliffe. Tawana Roberts writes in a *News-Herald* article, "Richard M. Hollingshead designed the first outdoor automobile theater in 1933 after concluding that people often did not go to the movies because they didn't always want to get dressed up and go out."

And from the very beginning, outdoor car theaters were promoted as a tempting alternative to the conventional "hardtop" theaters. They were popular among young people, who were able to cram their friends into one car, and young families, who didn't have to pay for a babysitter (particularly the large, and growing, baby boomer families). They could just bring their babies and children right along for the adventure, allowing more flexibility than an indoor theater.

Although drive-in theaters started popping up in the 1940s, they really took off in the 1950s. By 1958, there were more than four thousand drive-in theaters across the nation.

The Skyway Drive-In opened around 1950 at 7431 North Ridge Road in North Madison. It had one screen and enough space for up to three hundred cars. It was rebuilt in July 1966 after a fire ripped through it a month earlier and was closed after the 1989 season.

According to Dan Maxson's article "Lost Lake County Drive-Ins," "The Belvedere Drive-In, was located on the Morrison Farm (Girdled and Ravenna Road) south of the tracks." It opened in the late 1940s and closed just before the 1954 season. Many remember that the screen was set on a slant, on an uphill slope (golf course two for Quail Hollow). "Between the resulting wind-tunnel effect it created and driving up the hill to get to the parking area, the complications eventually led to its demise as the screen fell several times," writes Maxson.

The drive-in created other concerns, too; since the screen could be easily seen from Route 44, some claimed it could distract drivers. Maxson continues,

> *Others worried about kids sneaking in to watch "risky movies." Perhaps the most colorful anecdote, reported by Rose Moore, was the time a gangster movie kept Doris Morrison awake all night due to the sounds of auto chases, sirens and gunfire. All-in-all though, rural Concord and the surrounding neighborhood accepted the theater without much fuss. The former site remained popular for many years as a sledding spot, the tattered screen a mere backdrop of a moment in time.*

Mentor Twin Drive-In opened in 1949 at 9200 Mentor Avenue. Two thousand people attended opening night, with many cars being turned away, to enjoy *Blondie Knows Best*. According to the website Cinema Treasures, the drive-in was screening movies seven nights a week and took extra consideration for customers with babies, providing a free bottle-warming station and diaper service.

Mentor Amusement Company owned the drive-in, along with the Lake Theater and Park Theater in Painesville and the Lyric Theater in Fairport. The drive-in was originally supposed to be built right after World War II but was delayed three years because building materials were needed to construct new homes for returning veterans. Mentor Twin Drive-In had one of the first screen towers in the state built with steel rather than wood. It was designed in the shape of a triangle, allowing room for offices and storage at the base of the screen tower, and the screen was fifty-two by forty-two feet. (A wider, curved CinemaScope screen was later installed in front of the flat screen.) The drive-in became a twin theater in the late 1970s and closed in 1986. It was then demolished, and a Super Kmart was built on the site.

Back when a movie cost only seventy-five cents, many remember going to the drive-in on a first date, sneaking in from the field behind the drive-in, playing on the swings and merry-go-round before the movie began or working at the concession stand, selling popcorn and burgers. Some residents recall that people once reported seeing a lion walking around the Mentor drive-in, but after close inspection by law enforcement, it turned out to be a golden chow dog.

The Eastlake Drive-In, located at 34280 Vine Street, opened in 1950 with the premiere feature *A Ticket to Tomahawk*. It had one screen, concession stands and a playground and held up to five hundred cars. It closed in 1986 and was replaced by the Vineyards shopping plaza. Similarly, the Euclid Avenue Outdoor Theater opened at 28737 Euclid Avenue in 1948 with one screen and a seven-hundred-car capacity.

Now the closest drive-in theater remains outside the Lake County lines, in nearby Mayfield. The drive-ins may be gone, but the memory and nostalgia of this beloved summertime pastime remains.

ESCAPED CIRCUS ELEPHANT

"Escaped Circus Elephant Captured" was the headline of an Associated Press story on February 16, 1998. Tonya, the two-ton circus performer, escaped from the Mentor High School (MHS) PTA circus, which was a huge annual event held over President's Day weekend for several decades.

Morgan Leyes (MHS class of 2000) was a student at the time. As a member of the Fighting Cardinals Marching Band, she played the opening of each circus performance, and she recalls the day the elephant got loose.

> *I was in the student center playing cards with my friends, waiting for the next show. I remember hearing a bunch of commotion and looked up to see a giant gray thing run by. It took off the door and bent the frame. I was also there when the zebra escaped into the crowd. It was a bad weekend for the circus.*

According to the AP article, Tonya panicked while in the school hallway and ran off, knocking her assistant trainer to the ground before opening a door with her trunk to flee the building. The police chased Tonya on foot and in squad cars. Sergeant Kevin Knight said at the time, "I've been here for 17 years, and it's the first time we've had an elephant on the loose."

Tonya's trainers and volunteers also joined the chase as Tonya galloped toward a Big Lots store. The trainer finally caught up with her, about a quarter mile away from the school, and was able to coax her into his truck.

Tonya's trainer, Bret Bronson, said she got upset after another elephant was startled by a clown and bumped into her, squeezing her against the wall. "She was just like a child lost in a mall," Bronson said at the time. "She panicked." Thankfully, no one was injured.

But this wasn't the only time the circus led to excitement. The three-ring circus was held in the school's gym and drew international performers.

Lee Silvi, retired Fairport Harbor fire chief, was a full-time firefighter and later a lieutenant/safety officer for the Mentor Fire Department (FD). He was assigned to the Mentor FD Fire Prevention Bureau for several years too, as a certified fire safety inspector.

Because the circus was such a huge event (with the high school gym at full capacity), two fire inspectors worked every show in case there was a fire alarm or medical emergency. Silvi says for the years he was involved as Mentor FD at the shows, the circus was hosted by the Mentor PTA, which shared the profits with promoter George Hubler International Circus (based out of Dayton).

"George hired international acts some years, such as the Wallendas, and many, many others," explained Silvi. "It was a big operation, and depending on the year could include elephants, lions and/or tigers and so much more. He had a full-time announcer who traveled with him and a small circus stage band."

Silvi recalls a particularly memorable moment at the circus when a clown (who was a firefighter from Pennsylvania) was performing a circus act in a small clown car with a fire protection system installed in it that produced a cloud of carbon dioxide gas if there was a fire. Said Silvi,

> *He proved it worked. At one show there was a flash fire, and he activated the system, and I ran out with a fire extinguisher. The fire was NOT a planned part of the act, but after the show some of the spectators told me it was cool the two firefighters on duty were part of the act. (We were NOT part of the "act," and it took me awhile for my heartbeat to return to normal.)*

Silvi remembers that many in attendance jumped to their feet, cheered and clapped at the act. Luckily, he happened to have a fire extinguisher in hand, since it was a new act, and the fire protection installed in the car was effective, but the clown voluntarily did not do the act again for the rest of the shows. The circus is no longer held at the high school.

Chapter 8

ESTATES

PARMLY MANSION

The Parmly mansion, built in 1834 as a summer home, remains standing next to Perry Township Park. It was one of the most elegant homes in the area in its day, and ghost stories and legends surround it, according to Mary L. Platko's *A Little Bit of Perry History*. The Parmly family (formerly spelled Parmelee) came from Vermont, with the first member settling on River Road in Perry in 1814. Other family members followed, purchasing land on the lakeshores of Perry Township. They were successful in farming and other ventures, and the family at one point owned six thousand acres of nearby land.

Jehiel (sometimes written Jahiel) Parmly was said to be an abolitionist, helping slaves escape to freedom across Lake Erie to Canada. His mansion, with its ideal location on the lake, played a role in the Underground Railroad prior to the Civil War. According to legend, slaves were kept in the basement, hidden from the family's frequent prominent visitors. A lookout stayed on the high bank at night, watching for signals from boats arriving from Canada, and slaves were reportedly led from a tunnel in the basement of the mansion that led directly to the lakeshore.

Jehiel, who built the mansion, was a dentist, the profession chosen by eighteen members of his family. (Robert Ripley even included this fact in his *Believe It or Not* book.)

The Parmly mansion in Perry. *Courtesy of Jack Kless/Perry Historical Society.*

Jehiel's son Levi Spear Parmly left the family farm when he was twenty-two after an argument over how to hoe potatoes, saying, "This is the last row of potatoes I'll ever hoe." He headed to Boston, where he worked as a dentist's assistant. He and his brother Jehiel later wandered the battlefields of Lundy's Lane (present-day Niagara Falls, Ontario) in the War of 1812, gathering teeth from the skulls of soldiers to study.

By 1815, he was recommending that people clean their teeth by passing a piece of silk thread between them, emphasizing the importance of his new floss in a book called *A Practical Guide to the Management of Teeth*. He became known as the "Father of Preventative Dentistry."

The idea began to catch on, and years later in 1882, the Codman and Shurtleft Company began manufacturing unwaxed silk dental floss. Nearly two decades after that, Johnson and Johnson earned a patent for dental floss, introducing it to the masses.

The Parmly House in Perry was remodeled in 1916 to be used for Camp Roosevelt, which prepared boys to serve as soldiers in World War I.

As for the ghost stories, some believe Parmly haunts his old mansion. According to one legend, a group of slaves thought Parmly was a slave owner himself and feared he would turn them over to federal agents or return them to the South. So, as the story goes, late one night they escaped from the basement and murdered him. However, Eva Robbins Mallory, who lived in the mansion with her family between 1904 and 1913, thought perhaps the ghost stories evolved from visitors to the home who saw the animal skeletons and teeth that Dr. Parmly kept in his second-floor dentist's office.

Dorothy Bailey, who once lived in the mansion with her family, said they often heard loud thumps and doors opening and closing, but her mother believed there was no need to be afraid, because the ghosts were friendly.

The Perry Community Center building, overlooking Lake Erie, was built in recent years and sits on the grounds of the former Camp Roosevelt.

Another family member and dentist, Dr. Eleazer Parmly, opened the Parmly House Hotel in Painesville in 1861. Eleazer was one of the most widely traveled family members, living and/or practicing in several big cities, including Montreal; Boston; London; New York City; Washington; Shewsbury, New Jersey; and, of course, Perry.

According to the Family Parmelee website, Kelly Searsmith, whose grandmother worked as a clerk at the hotel, recalled riding up and down in the old-fashioned elevator and said the Von Trapp family (the inspiration for *The Sound of Music*) once stayed at the famed hotel.

An old advertisement states that rooms started at just a dollar a stay: "Modern equipment throughout. Many rooms with baths. The popular resort of more Sunday motor parties than any other hotel near Cleveland."

The hotel was torn down in the 1970s to make way for a downtown shop and office complex.

PARMLY HOTEL, PAINESVILLE, OHIO.

Postcard of the Parmly Hotel, Painesville, 1936. *Author's collection.*

HARKNESS ESTATE

In the late 1800s, when Eastlake became a summer playground for Cleveland millionaires, Stephen V. Harkness, a Standard Oil partner of John D. Rockefeller, purchased 222 acres by the mouth of the Chagrin River for about $100,000.

Several years earlier, he had built the Harkness block at Euclid Avenue and East Fifty-Fifth Street in Cleveland, and he was director of Euclid Avenue National Bank and Ohio River Railway Company and president of Iron Belt Mining Company and Cleveland Arcade Company.

According to the Eastlake Historical Society, Harkness built a three-story, twenty-four-room mansion with two huge stone pillars, a porch wrapping around three sides, solid mahogany doors, high ceilings and a fireplace in almost every room.

An ornamental coach house sheltered trotting horses, surreys and phaeton carriages. Five gas wells provided illumination for the mansion and outbuilding. The lands were beautifully landscaped, and Harkness even

Harkness Estate in Eastlake. *Courtesy of Eastlake Historical Society.*

The *Peerless*. *Courtesy of Little Red Schoolhouse.*

prevented erosion by having spiles driven in the form of jetties and docks and installing an elaborate system of drainage.

Harkness lived in the house with his second wife, Anna, and their three children, Charles, Edward and Florence.

The yacht *Peerless*, with anchorage in the Chagrin River, was purchased by Harkness in 1880 for $80,000. It held one-hundred-plus crew members and "exemplified the pretentious lifestyle enjoyed by these wealthy 'rusticators,'" according to research materials found in the Eastlake Historical Society.

CAMP HARKNESS

By the 1930s, when the Harkness family was no longer living on the estate, it had become a clean air camp called Camp Harkness.

Church congregations began showing photo slides titled "A Playground for the Children of the City" to encourage them to raise money to send children to Camp Harkness.

Photo of the senior girls at Harkness camp in Eastlake, 1937. *Courtesy of Eastlake Historical Society.*

The script for one of the slides reads: "In a backyard playground, dusty, dirty…the children of the city get exercise…but little of the vigor & inspiration of clean air…In summer camps such as Camp Harkness, near Cleveland, Ohio, a start is being made in giving the children of the city the right sort of recreation."

The camp had small cabins, plenty of room to run and explore, a kitchen and a dining hall. It even had its own Harkness Song, as printed in the 1938 "Century of Harkness Banquet" program:

> *We're from Harkness, we're from Harkness,*
> *We're from Harkness Camp.*
> *Where the water's wet and the dew is damp.*
> *We just love it, we just love it,*
> *And we've always got a grin,*
> *Come on you campers, let the fun begin!*
> *H-A-R-K-N-E-S-S!*

In 1950, Cleveland Electric Illuminated Company (CEI) removed all buildings from the Harkness land and constructed the Eastlake Power Plant, at a cost of $20 million.

The Fay Estate

A History of Surfside, written in 1987, found in the Eastlake Historical Society, says the section of Eastlake known as Surfside once contained apple orchards and a small airport.

> *The Fay Estate was a large tract of land which included fruit trees. This orchard has since been replaced by present-day East and West Overlook Drives. Apartments have been constructed on property owned by Dr. George Reeves. Another farm, the Meinkes, owned the airport where Eastlake Middle School and Hillcrest Drive is now located.*

The research materials go on to say that Surfside grew up around several streets that had been built as summer cottage areas, including Pinehurst (built well before Eastlake became a village in 1948), Parkway and the "Willoway Allottment," which includes present-day Traymore Boulevard, Courtland Boulevard, and Plymouth Drive.

Approximately 236 acres of farmland belonging to Willoughby families were purchased by Rex Land Company in 1957 and separated into nine hundred lots.

The small lakeside village of Timberlake lies to the west, and the September/October 1949 *Timberlake Times* recalls memories of late summer in the community:

> *We know it was way back when, but we did have a Beach party back there in August that hasn't been reported via the T. Times to date. If you didn't come along and join us then you surely must have heard us Whippenpoofing and Mill-streaming. Everybody brought their own fixin's, the fire was hot and donducive [sic]!!! The air was cool and the water was delightful. What with the jabbering clown and harmonizing we did have fun.*

Chandler Estate

More than a century ago, Elgercon, a sprawling property overlooking the Chagrin River valley to the south, was passed down to Gertrude Chandler Tucker. According to the Willoughby Historical Society, her father, Harrison T. Chandler, was born in Chandlerville, Illinois, in 1840, and after serving in the army during the Civil War, he became interested in banking. He was head of a Chandlerville bank for a decade, married Ellen Frances Foster and they had two daughters: Gertrude, born in 1872, and Constance, born in 1886.

The family moved to Euclid Avenue in Cleveland in 1881. Harrison bought an interest in Cleveland Type Foundry and was one of its officers for three years. He then formed Chandler and Price, with mechanic William T. Price, to manufacture printing machinery, which helped build the Chandler fortune. In 1900, the family bought seventy-one acres of land in Willoughby, which became known as the Chandler estate.

Harrison was president of the corporation until he died on January 1, 1912. His wife, Ellen, died one month later.

After inheriting the property, Gertrude and her husband, Stanley Tucker, built a stone mansion facing Ridge Road and bought land in the valley, now Lake Metropark's Gully Brook. They transported materials from Cleveland by train and horse and wagon to build the mansion, stables, carriage houses, garages, greenhouse and gardens.

The animal-loving family also had their own pet cemetery, still visible today, including headstones—now broken by time and vandals—and a metal arch (possibly once part of the garden) grown into the middle of a tree.

When Gertrude died in 1953, the estate was left to Western Reserve University, but a title transfer in 1954 allowed the Willoughby-Eastlake school system to buy the mansion and a large portion of the property. According to Dan Maxson's *Local Lore* blog, twenty rooms in the mansion became classrooms for two hundred elementary students, and a caretaker's home became the Sunny Lane School for children with disabilities. Other buildings on the site housed the Red Cross, industrial art classes and a nursing school.

By the late 1950s and early '60s, Chandler Road was renamed Shankland Road; the YMCA, high school and middle school were built on the property; and the Little Red Schoolhouse was moved there.

In recent years, the grand Chandler-Tucker estate was home to the Willoughby-Eastlake Board of Education, which was sadly destroyed by fire on a cold March night in 2017.

WKYC reported, "Willoughby Fire Chief Todd Ungar said two floors of the building were already engulfed when they arrived. He added that the first fire hydrant they tried to use was frozen and they were limited to the 500 gallons of water they had on the fire trucks. School officials say firefighters battled the blaze inside the building for 40 minutes before evacuating because the building had become unstable." There were no injuries, but computers, documents and historic photos of the building were destroyed.

Today, several of the barns and structures remain on the property, including original printing presses.

Wickliffe's "Millionaire's Mile"

Cleveland was known for having Millionaire's Row, but Wickliffe had its own Millionaire's Mile. By the late 1800s, Ridge Road was lined with beautiful summer estates.

Rockefeller

Franklin Rockefeller, brother of John D. Rockefeller, who was a business magnate, philanthropist and, at one time, the richest person in the country, built his estate, named "Lakeland," south of Ridge Road in Wickliffe.

Franklin was born in 1845 in New York and enlisted at sixteen years old to fight in the Civil War. In 1870, he married Helen Scofield, and they had five children.

Lakeland, which faced Ridge Road, sat about five hundred feet back. The 158-acre property included a large barn, a sheep house, a racetrack, a pool and a high stone wall. It even had its own interurban line extension up Rockefeller Road for family and friends.

Franklin died in Cleveland in 1917, and his widow sold the property in 1925 for $200,000.

Years later, Wickliffe Senior High School was built on a portion of Rockfeller's estate, and the Wickliffe Board of Education operates out of the former carriage house.

Squire's Castle/Cobblestone Garth

Fergus Bowden Squire (whom many know for his home, Squire's Castle, in Willoughby Hills) also built an estate in Wickliffe, known as Cobblestone Garth. It was across the ridge from Wickliffe City Hall, which was Harry Coulby's mansion, Coulallenby.

Postcard of Cobblestone Garth in Wickliffe, 1907. *Courtesy of Willoughby Historical Society.*

Squire (often referred to as F.B. Squire) was born in Devon, in southwest England, in 1850. He and his family immigrated to the United States in 1860 and settled in Cleveland. When Squire was only fifteen years old, he left school to work at a local paper mill but ended up leaving to work at an oil refinery, Alexander, Scofield & Company. While there, he was taught at night by private tutors and worked his way up to bookkeeper.

Squire eventually formed Newman, Squire & Company, which developed a horse-drawn oil tanker, and formed the Cleveland Bulk Oil Company, the first company in the United States to deliver refined petroleum right to retail customers' doors. He then joined Standard Oil Company, on the East Coast, as an inspector for oil shipments leaving the country and executive for several years before returning to Cleveland after retiring from Standard Oil for the first time.

He and his wife, Louisa Breymaier Squire, lived on Prospect Avenue and later Euclid Avenue's Millionaire's Row at East Seventy-Eighth Street. He joined Standard Oil as a top executive again in 1880, rose to secretary and became quite wealthy.

In 1890, attracted by the beauty of the Chagrin Valley, Squire bought 525 acres of land, with plans to construct two buildings in the style of English or German baronial halls. The Squire's Castle part of the Cleveland Metroparks system that we know today wasn't built to be Squire's home but the gatehouse and caretaker's quarters. The castle-like structure was made of Euclid bluestone, quarried in what is now the Metroparks Euclid Creek Reservation.

Squire planned to call his home River Farm Estate and began planting groves of trees and adding roads, bridges and ponds (like Sunset Pond, just two miles away from the castle). However, his wife hated the idea of living in the country, so the main house was never built.

The Squires built their second country home a little closer to Cleveland on Ridge Road in Wickliffe around 1900, naming it Cobblestone Garth. It was built in a Victorian style, mainly out of wood, and filled with modern conveniences. A year after it was completed in 1902, it was featured in *The Country Estates of Cleveland Men*. The Squires moved to Cobblestone Garth permanently in 1911. (Most of Cobblestone Garth was torn down years later, but the stone border wall, gatehouse and unique lighthouse structure remain on the property, across from Coulby Park).

Squire's Castle, with windows and a dormer on the front roof, circa 1930. *Courtesy of Willoughby Historical Society.*

Squire continued to use the castle as a weekend getaway, and his daughter Irma sometimes accompanied him. The castle had several living areas and bedrooms, along with a large kitchen and breakfast porch and a library filled with books, paintings and taxidermy animals from his many hunting expeditions. The rooms had white plaster walls and leaded glass windows, allowing the Squires to gaze out at their stunning property, yet the castle was also rustic and didn't have electricity, natural gas, a sewer or running water.

In the early 1920s, Squire sold the castle and land to a private developer, and the Cleveland Park Board (precursor to the Cleveland Metroparks) acquired it in 1925. At this time, visitors to the park began referring to it as Squire's Castle. Over time, the castle was vandalized, and to keep the structure safe for park visitors, it was stripped of whatever wasn't already removed, such as doors and window glass, floors and woodwork. Even the basement was filled in. Remnants of the castle shell include iron struts that supported the second and third floors and mounting holes that held the leaded glass windows.

Squire's Castle is the inspiration for ghost stories and urban legends, like that of a floating orb, or a lit lantern, reportedly seen in the top of the castle, said to be the ghost of Mrs. Squire, who fell down the stairs, broke her neck and died in the castle. This, of course, never happened, since she went on to live until 1927, after the Chagrin Valley property was sold, and died of pneumonia at Cobblestone Garth in Wickliffe. Her husband died five years later.

For most who visit the castle, like my own family, it is a place that brings happiness. It's a chance for children to let their imaginations run wild as they roam a true castle as kings and queens and race across its lawn, for hikers to climb up the inclined trails behind the structure and for special photos to be taken for proms, high school graduations and weddings.

Although the castle never lived up to its full potential for the Squires, it has been a place of beauty and intrigue enjoyed by northeast Ohioans for decades.

Chapter 9

HEROES, INVENTORS AND LEGENDARY RESIDENTS

We live in a heroic age. Not seldom are we thrilled by deeds of heroism where men or women are injured or lose their lives in attempting to preserve or rescue their fellows.
—Andrew Carnegie, 1904

CARNEGIE HERO SHELDON JOSEPH HARRIS

Sheldon Joseph Harris was born in Sandy Creek, New York, on December 4, 1903. His granddaughter, Katherine Harris Szerdy, says he was a natural-born swimmer, enlisted in the U.S. Coast Guard and was later stationed in Fairport Harbor. He was a rescue diver before oxygen tanks were used and was said to be able to hold his breath for a very long time.

Katherine says her grandfather was known to be a bit of a rebel and had trouble following orders. She says it's an inherited trait. According to family legend, Sheldon's dad, George, once tried enlisting in the army during the Civil War when he was thirteen years old, with his thirty-one-year-old father. "My great-grandfather was so tall, and lied about his age, but when they found out they took him off the front line and made him a drummer boy."

After serving about a year, Sheldon was honorably discharged from the Coast Guard for unknown reasons. In 1927, he married Katherine Helen Warner, whose family worked for Storrs and Harrison Nursery, and they

Postcard of the Coast Guard station in Fairport, Ohio. *Author's collection*.

Sheldon Joseph Harris (*second from left*) and his Coast Guard mates, 1920s. *Courtesy of Katherine Harris Szerdy*.

bought a home at 2580 Hale Road, farming several acres of land. Sheldon then started working for the Cleveland Electric Illuminating Company.

"He had a real dangerous job," explained Katherine. "The fact that he became a rescue diver and a lineman for the illuminating company, I just think he must have been a risk-taker. He didn't mind risking his life for others."

On August 20, 1930, twenty-six-year-old Sheldon took the ultimate risk. He and twenty-one-year-old Kenneth C. Collier were installing a "jumper" on a high-tension line, east of Painesville, near the New York Central tracks. A newspaper clipping from the time reported:

> *Ten feet below was a steel cross arm to which high voltage wires were attached. Collier climbed to the lower cross arm and as he held to a guy wire received the shock. Harris saw his plight and descended to strike repeatedly at Collier who was finally knocked to the ground.*

Collier died from a fractured skull when he hit the ground, and Sheldon was killed instantly when thirty-three thousand volts of electricity passed through his body.

Illuminating Company employees saw everything while standing at the foot of the pole. "They saw Harris beating Collier's arms in an effort to release him, and a moment later, when Collier fell, they tried to catch him. When they looked up again Harris' body was hanging limply from the line, with one of his gloves in flames."

Sheldon died a hero's death and was posthumously cited for his heroism by the Carnegie Hero Fund Commission. His widow, who had just learned she was pregnant with their second child (Pauline), was awarded a bronze medal and twenty-five dollars a month in death benefits. Their first child, Stanley (Katherine's father), was just thirteen months old.

The Carnegie Medal, created by steelmaker Andrew Carnegie in 1904 after a coal mine disaster in the suburbs of Pittsburgh, is still awarded today, to recognize and support those who perform acts of heroism in civilian life in the United States and Canada. Carnegie wanted to "bring to light the good deeds of those acting on behalf of their fellow man," according to the Carnegie Hero Fund Commission Website.

About 10 percent of nominees are awarded medals, and Sheldon is one of nine recipients from Lake County, according to the Carnegie Hero archives.

Lake County Andrew Carnegie Medal Recipients

In 1909, fifteen-year-old Edward T. Rasmussen saved thirty-seven-year-old Henry M. Merritt when he fell from a pier into the Grand River.

In 1927, thirty-two-year-old George Lyle Tribby died attempting to save Mary A. Royal, twenty-three, who got caught in a strong current after falling off a break wall into Lake Erie.

In 1936, James W. Marble, thirty-two, assistant manager of a gasoline and oil company in Willoughby, saved the company president, sixty-four-year-old William A. Johnson, from burning, following an explosion after Johnson lowered a lighted lantern into a large tank of drained gasoline.

In 1967, Michael L. Kessler, twenty-one, helped save Robert T. Carter, fourteen, from suffocating when he was overcome by fumes while spraying aluminum paint in an abandoned belowground cistern.

In 1969, in Willowick, Francis J. O'Hara, thirteen, died helping to save Steven A. DeSantis, fourteen, from drowning when a large section of ice broke away while they were walking along the ice-covered shore of Lake Erie.

In 2016, police officers Robert Prochazka, forty-nine, and Christopher M. Olup, thirty-four, saved Thomas C. Haley, fifty-four, from burning in his Willowick home; both officers entered as smoke poured out and dragged Haley to safety.

In 2020, Shane Morris, fifteen, jumped into Lake Erie, near Mentor, to save thirteen-year-old Donovan Conwell, who was drifting into deep water. Authorities arrived in a boat and took them to safety.

Civil War Medal of Honor Recipient
Albert Clapp

In 1860, Mentor resident Albert A. Clapp was a nineteen-year-old student at the Western Reserve Eclectic Institute in Hiram, Ohio. One year later, when the Civil War began, he was among the first to enlist as a soldier in the Second Cavalry.

According to Thomas Matowitz, author of *Mentor*, on April 6, 1865, at the Battle of Sailor's Creek, in Virginia, Clapp rode into the ranks of the Eighth Florida and captured the unit's battle flag. At the site, which is now a state park, more than 7,700 soldiers in Confederate general Robert E. Lee's army were killed, wounded or captured. Clapp was later awarded the Medal of Honor for his bravery from Secretary of War Edwin M. Stanton.

In total, Clapp, impressively, served in seventeen of the regiment's battles and was even present, several days later, on April 9, 1865, when General Lee surrendered his twenty-eight thousand troops to Union General Ulysses S. Grant at the Appomattox Court House, in Virginia. It was a pivotal moment known to be the catalyst to end the Civil War.

An article by Matowitz on the City of Mentor's website says Clapp returned to Mentor in the summer of 1865, and became a farmer. He married Cynthia Bissell, from Painesville, and they had five sons. They left Mentor in 1873 and headed west to California, where he lived the rest of his days.

Journalist/Adventurer Walter Wellman

Walter Wellman, born in Concord in 1858, became a journalist, explorer and adventurer. He married Laura McCann, of Canton, in 1878 and founded the *Cincinnati Post* when he was twenty-one years old. He built a dirigible named *Polar Expedition* in 1905, with the goal of reaching the North Pole ahead of famed explorer Robert Peary (who was attempting to reach it by dogsled). "Adventure for mere adventure sake is always worthwhile," Peary once wrote.

According to Daniel Maxson and Debra L. Bechel-Esker in *Concord Township*, Wellman was the first person to attempt to cross the Atlantic Ocean by air. In 1910, he piloted the dirigible *America* with a new "equilibrator" feature designed to keep the ship within two hundred feet of the water. However, he had to abandon ship four hundred miles off Cape Hatteras. Wellman and his crew made several other attempts flying dirigibles, but many ended in disaster. His last attempt, which resulted in the deaths of the crew, ended his adventures.

The remains of his last dirigible were donated to the Smithsonian Institution. Wellman, often called the Lindbergh of his day, died in 1934.

Walter Wellman on the deck of the dirigible *Polar Expedition*. Printed in the *Chicago Record-Herald*, circa 1907–10. *Courtesy of Library of Congress.*

FARMER/INVENTOR JOHN CZ

On a crisp autumn night, moonlight shines down on the twirling, twisting vines of a pumpkin patch in North Madison, revealing the unusually shaped gourds below. They were grown, by an inventive farmer, to look like human heads.

In the 1930s, John M. Czeszcziczki (known as John Cz) had the creepiest pumpkin patch in town. On his Dock Road farm, he spent four years experimenting with several materials—including iron, lead, glass (which broke), bronze, concrete and aluminum—to create a pumpkin mold.

First, he shaped human heads in plaster, made metal molds from the forms, then encased a small pumpkin, about the size of a grapefruit, on the vine in a mold. It took on the shape of the mold during its initial fifteen-day growth phase, and when Cz removed the mold, the pumpkin continued to grow larger, retaining the shape. According to local legend, neighbors could sometimes hear the sharp explosions of iron molds bursting open under the pressure of the growing pumpkins, as human-like pumpkin heads popped out.

John Cz, of Madison, in his pumpkin field with his molded pumpkins. *Courtesy of Art and Pat Cz Stafford.*

John Cz creating faces on his molded pumpkins. *Courtesy of Art and Pat Cz Stafford.*

Cz later patented several types of aluminum molds, which held up better than iron, and made some look like celebrities, including Clark Gable, Greta Garbo and President Roosevelt. He gave his pumpkins lifelike appearances by painting on eyes and other features or adding corn teeth and a mustache made from corn silk.

Cz's hobby brought him international fame, and he made headlines around the globe; a German magazine even ran a feature story on his growing methods. He received letters from all over the United States, and in 1938 he received an invitation, and round-trip railroad ticket, to appear on Dave Elman's *Hobby Lobby* radio program in New York City.

Some of Cz's creations sold for ten to fifty dollars, a very large sum in the 1930s. He planned to market his last invention—a plastic mold, which was lighter and cheaper than aluminum—through magazine ads, so everyone could have the fun of growing pumpkins with faces. However, after a decade of growing his unique pumpkins, Cz packed away his molds to focus on his duties of operating a large farm.

Cz died in 1984, and two years later, David Pethtel bought Cz's farm. While walking through the overgrown grass and fields that had been neglected for years, he was surprised to stumble upon a pile of metal objects shaped like human heads. Although they were aged and covered in grime, he soon discovered they were pieces of lost Lake County history.

According to the Madison Historical Society, Harold Rutter is the current owner of Cz's property (as of 2021). His dog dug up a lead pumpkin mask, believed to be an early prototype, as it's not as refined as Cz's later masks.

There is no record that Cz ever sold any of his masks; however, his son said he used to hang them on the inside of their barn. It's believed that, over time, people took them from his property, and now they are prized by collectors in Madison and the surrounding region; some have even sold for several hundred dollars.

In 2021, the Madison Historical Society showcased the inventions of John Cz. It was the first time several of his masks (including the iron prototype and aluminum and plastic molds), photos and newspaper articles were displayed in one place.

Shepherdess Dorothea Davis

Growing up in Lake County, I often passed a stretch of land on the south side of Euclid Avenue in Willoughby, thick with trees and rolling hills, with a natural spring that meandered through the bottom of a ravine. Of course, the land stood out amid a suburban business district of strip malls and apartment buildings, but it was the many sheep, and their shepherdess, Dorothea Davis, who were the stars.

According to author Dr. Nancymarie Phillips's *The Song of the Shepherdess*, Dorothea was born in 1913, the first of four daughters, to Manyard and Elizabeth Davis. The family lived in the same house where her father, Maynard, was born in 1883. The farm's postal address, as of the 1940s, was 28½ Euclid Avenue, Wickliffe, and most recently became 34000 Euclid Avenue, Willoughby. "The area's boundary lines changed six times making it the only city in Ohio to have changed county affiliations so many times."

Many trees on the property were even imported from England—with some reportedly remaining today, even though, after Dorothea's death in 2003, her property was cleared to make room for a residential stretch of condominiums called Shepherd's Glen.

Dorothea Davis with her sheep, Gemini. *Courtesy of Nancymarie Phillips.*

Dorothea graduated from Willoughby Union High School in 1931 and was the only one of her sisters not to graduate from college, sacrificing her graduation when money was tight. For many years, she was a beloved librarian, working at the Willoughby Library from 1950 to 1978, when she retired.

Phillips lived next door to Dorothea and became friends with her over the span of seven years. She says Dorothea got her first lamb as a pet when she was in her thirties or forties and the next about a decade later, and they quickly multiplied. She says Dorothea loved, and named, every sheep on her property, and she remembers Dorothea fondly as being very gentle, spiritual and in touch with nature. It was that gentle spirit that was hurt by the very name many people knew her by: "the sheep lady." Phillips says Dorothea preferred to be called by her real name or even "the shepherdess."

Around 1997, Dorothea began sharing her family stories with Nancymarie, who suggested she write them down. But Dorothea declined, saying she preferred to write poetry. Dorothea asked Phillips, a published author, to write a book about her life, which Dorothea named herself: *The Song of the Shepherdess*.

Once, when Dorothea and Nancymarie were about to enjoy dinner together, Dorothea asked Nancymarie if she would like her to say grace. Dorothea recited a poem that she wrote called "In the Barn":

> *Have you ever seen a little lamb just a few hours old?*
> *All snug and warm inside the barn safe from the wind and cold.*
> *Have you ever heard her soft, sweet voice and her mother's guttural reply?*
> *Used only when her babe is new, just like a loving sigh.*
> *'Tis then you know that God is there, his gentle arms do hold*
> *Every one of his own lambs, kept safe within the fold. Amen.*

Nancymarie remembers Dorothea's entire property was filled with beauty, the kind you might normally overlook, like a special tree, which remains today, brought over from England. It looked like someone had carved a heart into the top, but it was the natural formation left by a fallen branch. Natural springs and gas wells also dotted the property.

Dorothea referred to her sheep, which started out as Shropshires but blended to a Babydoll breed over the years, as her lambies and babies. They were often seen standing on bales of hay and grazing along the wooden fence on her property, just feet away from traffic whizzing by. Sometimes the sheep even wandered off the property, ending up on the busy street.

Although Dorothea was approached repeatedly to sell her valuable land to developers, she always stood her ground and stayed on her 13½-acre family farm. Dorothea lived until she was ninety years old, when she had a heart attack and died while climbing up the ravine on her beloved property after rescuing a ram that fell down it and got stuck in old fencing. It was her last act of selfless love for her lambies.

Not much remains of Dorothea's farm except the natural spring and a plaque, dedicated by Sheperd's Glen, standing on her former property in her honor.

Dorothea's legacy will always be an important part of the community: her love of children and books as a librarian, her compassion for animals and nature as a shepherdess and her strong will as a property owner to preserve her family's history and live on her own terms among an ever-changing landscape.

DUKE THE DOG FIREMAN

Duke, the English collie, was curled up fast asleep on a crisp fall morning in Perry Village. In an instant, he was awoken from his slumber by the smell of acrid smoke in the air and shouts of "Fire!"

On September 28, 1909, at 5:45 a.m., Jim Murphy walked out the back door of his home, on what is now Main Street in Perry Village, and saw smoke and flames shooting through the sides of a shed in the rear of the Langshaw's stores. The shed stored oil, which quickly ignited the blaze that burned through the business block on the east side of Main Street and became known as the Great Perry Fire (believed to be the worst in the community to that date).

According to Mary Platko's *A Little Bit of Perry History*, the burned buildings included F.W. Langshaw's General Merchandise Store and Meat Market and barn, the Perry Telephone Exchange over the market, the Perry Post Office, dwellings owned by Mrs. F.G. Salkeld and F.W. Langshaw, Orcutt warehouse and barn and William Northhard's barn.

The shouts of "Fire!" quickly awakened the sleepy residents, and they fought the blaze with a fire bucket brigade, because there was no organized fire department in Perry at the time. People who kept fire buckets ready

Duke the fire dog. *Courtesy of Jack Kless/Perry Historical Society.*

The Great Perry Fire, September 28, 1909. *Courtesy of Jack Kless/Perry Historical Society.*

in their homes for any fire emergencies brought the buckets to the scene and tried their best to douse the flames. However, it wasn't enough, so the Madison and Painesville fire departments were called in to help. Mary Platko writes,

> *Earnest Pancost was early at the fire and kicked in the door of the post office and with the assistance of others saved all the mail matter in that*

office. Others broke in the doors of the stores, but it was impossible to save anything from them except the account books.

In stepped Duke, who quickly became a legendary hero to the residents of Perry Village.

The *Telegraph Republican*, of Painesville, covered the big news of the fire that day and included a separate front-page article written about Duke, the "dog fireman." The story reads:

One of the unusual features of the fire was a dog fireman. "Duke," an English collie purchased in England by Page Craine, Alaskan explorer and proprietor of "The Curiosity Shop," put the intelligent animal to work early in the history of the blaze. Harnessed by Eskimo sled rigging to a four-wheeled cart, the dog rushed back and forth from the town wells to the scene of the fire and did great service. On the wagon were carried several large cans of water and the dog was able to draw 300 pounds at a trip without the slightest effort. In fact, the dog is capable of hauling nine times its own weight. The animal is a beautiful specimen of collie. It seemed to think that the role of fireman was the greatest sport in the world and no horse could have done better.

The total loss to the businesses of the village from the destructive fire was between $25,000 and $30,000. It likely would have been far worse had it not been for the heroic efforts of the townspeople and Duke the dog fireman.

Chapter 10

TREASURES, COLLECTIBLES AND HEISTS

The Riverrock House

Fallingwater in Pennsylvania may be one of architect Frank Lloyd Wright's most famous projects, but the last home he designed before his death was to be built in Willoughby.

According to legend, in the 1950s, Louis (longtime high school and college art teacher and artist) and Pauline Penfield visited Frank Lloyd Wright's studio in Wisconsin. When Wright appeared while they were touring his drafting room, Louis asked if he could design a home for someone as tall as him (six feet eight inches).

Wright's response was that anyone as tall as Louis was a weed and that he'd have to build a machine to tip him sideways. He then turned and left. Six months later, the Penfields received a mailing tube containing a colored pencil rendering of a house designed for them by Wright. It had a high ceiling, stairs with wide steps and sixteen thin ribbon windows.

Penfield House, as it's known today, was built in 1955 on a rise overlooking the Chagrin River. The site was originally farmland with wheat fields and river bluffs in the distance. The house was situated so the Penfields could enjoy the expansive view.

Several years later, in 1957, when Wright was ninety-two years old, the Penfields commissioned him to design a second house, to be built several hundred feet south of the first home. When Wright died in 1959, the family

Penfield House, Willoughby. *Courtesy of Sarah Dykstra/Penfield House LLC.*

assumed they would never see the blueprints, but to their astonishment, a mailing tube arrived a week after Wright's funeral containing the drawing for their second home, which Wright called the "river rock house" after the stone with which it was to be built. It was on the drawing board when Wright died, designated as project number 5909, indicating it was the ninth house he designed in 1959. It was his last residential commission.

Although most of Wright's clients canceled their projects after his death, Penfield didn't; he hired William Wesley Peters to finish the blueprints and paid the architectural fee to Wright's foundation. Louis gathered stone from the Chagrin River for several years but only managed to build a few feet of one wall for a documentary he was creating.

The 10.67-acre lot remains vacant, waiting for Riverrock to be built. Even the poplar tree that Wright designated as the natural feature around which the house was to be built still stands. The Penfields no longer own the property, although it was in the hands of their son Paul for many years. He restored much of it by using black cherry trees that grew abundantly on the property.

Paul said that when the first design was completed, the Penfields were informed that freeway I-90 would be constructed right through where the house was to be built. Paul said John Sherwin, who lived across the river, started pulling up stakes that surveyors put in for the new highway, warning that it was a bad place to build because the ground was full of blue shale, which couldn't support the kind of bridge they were planning. The builders realized Sherwin was right and rerouted the project to the north.

Today, the Penfield house, the Riverrock blueprints and the property on which it is still waiting to be built are privately owned by someone who appreciates it just as much as the original owners and hopes to build Riverrock in the future.

GRAND RIVER TREASURE

Two miles from Lake Erie, near Fairport Harbor, on the west bank of the Grand River, lies nearly $800,000 in buried gold bars—that is, if you believe the legend. Many have tried to find the treasure, buried more than 150 years ago, yet no one has (admittedly) been successful.

It all started in 1862, when three men robbed a Canadian bank, fleeing with gold bars (then valued at around $50,000). They quickly escaped the country by boating across sixty miles of Lake Erie to Lake County, Ohio.

"The ride across the lake was nerve-wracking, to say the least. But it was now nearing an end. As the three watched the circular pattern from the Fairport Harbor lighthouse beacon, they knew they would simply follow it to shore and land the vessel with its precious cargo," reads Wendy Koile's *Legends and Lost Treasure of Northern Ohio*.

The men approached the shore, guiding their boat into the harbor, then paddling against the current down the Grand River, which empties into the lake, until they felt safe to land on the west bank about two miles down the river.

Although they had worked together to steal the treasure, they argued about how to divide it. As the story goes, the strongest of the three overtook his partners, killing them both and burying their bodies on the riverbank. He took two bullion bars for himself and buried the rest of the gold in the same spot, marking off the paces to his treasure, with plans to come back.

However, he never made it back to Ohio. Just months after the robbery, he lay dying in a hospital from pulmonary disease. He confessed the whole robbery to his nurse and doctor, saying the treasure could be found about two miles from the mouth of the Grand River, "Three feet deep and 30 paces northwest of a large oak tree on the riverbank."

His doctor, unsuccessfully, searched for the treasure, arriving by steamboat. He even sent a team of professionals the following year to try again. They didn't find the treasure, but their visit did stir up interest within the community, and as the story spread, so did the attempts to dig up the hidden gold.

In the following years, the base of every oak along the west bank of the river was searched. Sailors were even known to stealthily leave their ships and dig by moonlight. As a boy, a local remembers hunting for the treasure and seeing lanterns flickering among the trees as others scoured the area.

One of the many challenges in locating the treasure is that the course of the river, which twists throughout Grand River, Fairport Harbor and Painesville, has changed over time and is now different than it was in 1862.

In 1890, a body, believed to be that of one of the murdered robbers, was found on the banks of the Grand River. According to the coroner's report, the skeleton's skull had a huge hole in it, suggesting a strike to the head. The skeleton was never identified, and a second was never found.

THE MOUNDS CLUB

Another robbery that resulted in stolen treasure took place at present-day LaVera Party Center, on Chardon Road in Willoughby Hills. It's a popular venue for weddings and celebrations, but nearly a century ago it was the site of one of Lake County's biggest heists.

Thomas "Black Jack" McGinty built it as the Mounds Club in 1930. McGinty was known as Cleveland's biggest sports and gambling promoter and a member of the Cleveland Gang, an organized crime group that controlled gambling and other criminal activities during the 1930s and '40s, according to *Here Is Ohio's Lake County*.

The Mounds Club was a sophisticated nightclub known for its gambling and illegal liquor. It was also called "the lion's club" and had lion symbols all around, including murals on the walls, an elaborate gate at the entrance and statues on the front lawn.

Patrons could enjoy dinner and mixed drinks—even though it was said that the club did not hold a state license to serve liquor—and nationally known entertainment like Lena Horne and Dean Martin. In the 1930s and '40s, Lake County and state officials raided the Mounds Club at least three times but didn't find evidence of illegal alcohol or gambling.

One night, in late September 1947, about 250 people were in the club watching Peter Lind Hayes and his wife, Mary Healy, performing on stage when a group of men, wearing stocking masks and carrying submachine guns, entered the dining room.

> *Guests thought this was part of the show. Shots were fired into the ceiling. Guests were told to place money, jewelry and watches on the table. Robbers, referring to each other by numbers, proceeded to gather up the valuables using the tablecloths as bags. They also gathered money from the safe and cash drawers and left the area stealing three cars from the parking lot.*

More than $400,000 in jewelry and cash was stolen that night, and no one was ever charged in the robbery, although it was thought it may have been a rival of the Cleveland Gang.

Ohio governor Frank Lausche closed the Mounds Club in 1949, and the Cleveland Gang members who owned it sold it a year later, moved to Las Vegas and opened the Desert Inn.

PAINESVILLE NATIONAL BANK

Lake County is linked to some highly sought-after collectibles that reflect our region's past. Occasionally, a banknote from the Painesville National Bank shows up to buy online or at auction.

The Painesville National Bank was built by Jonathan Goldsmith; it opened as the Bank of Geauga in 1831 and was the third bank in the Western Reserve. The Bank of Geauga was located on Main Street in Painesville and became the Painesville National Bank after the passage of the National Bank Act of 1863, creating a system of banks with uniform national currency. In 1882, it was granted its first charter to issue six kinds of banknotes, including tens and twenties.

In 1925, the building was destroyed by a fire and rebuilt at a different location, where the Lake County Visitor's Bureau is today. The fire was said to have started in the basement, from an undetermined source. A March 2, 1925 edition of the *Painesville Telegraph* reads: "All the currency in the cashier cages was placed in safety. One man had his hand badly smashed attempting to close the door of the safety deposit vaults in the basement. The door was finally closed, and the records made safe from the flames and water."

A 4523a, Painesville National Bank, Painesville, O.

This looks more like W.Va. than any place I know of. Bill

Postcard of the Painesville National Bank, circa 1907. *Courtesy of Bill Smith.*

Haskell Fishing Lures

Haskell fishing lure. *Courtesy of Ron Gast, https://luresnreels.com.*

Arguably the most valuable fishing lure in the world, the Haskell Minnow, has ties to Lake County.

At ten inches in length, the Giant Haskell is considered extremely rare, at nearly double the size of other highly collectible Haskell Minnows. The fishing lures were named after lure maker Riley Haskell, who was born in Geauga County (before it became part of Lake County) in 1827. He grew up in Painesville, where fishing and lure making were more than just sports; they were a means of survival. Before making lures, Haskell was a gunsmith (and gun collectors also prize his creations).

In 1859, Haskell was granted a patent for his minnow-shaped lure constructed of ornate copper and brass, complete with eyes, fins, tail and scale pattern and stamped with his name and "Painesville." The inside of the metal body had cork in the top and lead in the bottom to keep the lure vertical in the water. Although the lures were made in several sizes, the larger varieties are the scarcest and most valuable.

Riley Haskell died in Mentor in 1882, at the age of fifty-five.

Interestingly, local historian Bill Smith discovered that Haskell used to also stamp coins of the day, including Indian-head pennies and Seated Liberty half dollars, with "Haskell" or "Riley Haskell, Painesville, O.," following the rising fame of his stamped lures. On its own, such a coin may only be worth a few dollars, but with the Haskell stamp, it could sell for hundreds more.

According to Major League Fishing, in 2003, Haskell's 1859 Giant Haskell minnow sold at auction for a world record $101,200.

"Nap" Lajoi

If you have an authentic Napoleon "Nap" Lajoie (pronounced lash'u-wā, with emphasis on the first syllable) baseball card, you're in luck, because it can sell for more than $1,000.

Lajoie, nicknamed "Nap" and "Larry" by those who had trouble pronouncing "Lajoie," was a hitter extraordinaire, a sublime fielder, a manager and an executive. He has been called "the first superstar in American League history" and was, at one time, a Lake County resident.

Lajoie, of French-Canadian descent, was born in Rhode Island in 1874. He first played baseball professionally in 1895, at twenty-one years old, when the Fall River team of the New England League offered him a contract. "When I told my father that I had decided to take the job he was very angry," Lajoie recalled. "He shouted that ballplayers were bums and that nobody respected them, but I was determined to give it a try at least one season."

Lajoie broke into the National League's Philadelphia Phillies a year later, hitting .326 in thirty-nine games. In 1901, he controversially signed with the Athletics in violation of the reserve clause. He played for the A's for one season before the league president transferred him to Cleveland to avoid a Pennsylvania court order that would have sent him back to the Phillies.

In Cleveland, Lajoie became the face of the fledgling club, known as the Bronchos, when they renamed themselves after him and became known as the Naps. Lajoie went on to hit over .300 in eleven of his first twelve seasons in Cleveland and won the first four American League batting crowns. He

Baseball players Napoleon Lajoie (*left*) and Fred Lake, circa 1908. *Courtesy of Library of Congress.*

was also the first American League player to be intentionally walked while the bases were fully loaded.

Lajoie was a player-manager for the Naps for several years but resigned to concentrate on playing and eventually returned to the Athletics at the end of his career. He was inducted into the National Baseball Hall of Fame in 1937, alongside other celebrated players like Cy Young. (Babe Ruth and Ty Cobb were inductees in the Hall of Fame's inaugural year in 1936.) Young once said, "Lajoie was one of the most rugged hitters I ever faced. He'd take your leg off with a line drive, turn the third baseman around like a swinging door, and powder the hand of the left fielder."

Local historian Bill Smith discovered that Nap and his wife, Myrtle, were listed in a Lake Country directory as living on Salida Drive in Mentor-on-the-Lake after his retirement, before moving to Florida in 1943. Myrtle died in 1951, and Nap died in 1959.

Nap's spirit and drive live on, inspiring generations through his impressive career and heartfelt words: "You don't always need stars to win. You don't always need greatness. Sometimes spirit, determination, fight will do as well."

EPILOGUE

Although through the years we've lost many of the industries Lake County was founded on, we still have pieces of our past to remind us of where we came from. Some businesses that began in simpler times, before the rise of retail and big box stores, have survived.

Joughin Hardware, in Painesville, has been an anchor in the community since 1877. The wooden floors have just the right amount of creak to remind you of the history embedded on every level. It's an unofficial museum of lost Lake County business and industry. Vintage and antique tools and original store fixtures (like a sliding wooden ladder and cash register) are scattered among the new items. A bag from the now defunct Nickel Plate Coal & Supply Company of Painesville that held "fireplace fuel" hangs on the wall. A receipt from the W. Bingham Company, in Cleveland, written out to "J.W. Joughin Hdwe," is preserved under glass, and rulers in display cases come from long-gone businesses like Mary Carter Paints on the Park in downtown Painesville and Willoughby Hardware Company.

Rudy's Quality Meats started in Cleveland in 1928 and opened in Willowick in the early 1960s. The Bukovec family, who still runs it, has known me since I was a kid shopping there with my parents and even fondly remembers when my grandparents were customers. It a local staple when it comes to high-quality cuts of meat and smoked sausage.

The smell of baked goods has lured customers into Gartman's Model Bakery, in Painesville, for more than a century. It opened in 1898 and has

Vintage postcard of Main Street, Painesville. *Author's collection.*

been owned by the Gartman family since 1917. It is still known for making baked goods by hand, like cassata cakes and German cheesecake.

These historic stores, bakeries and restaurants have survived and even thrived for so long because they know the key to success comes from old-fashioned values passed down through generations. Customers choose to shop in these businesses because they value hard work, a friendly face willing to help and the high-quality products that are still found within their walls.

The desire to preserve our past is in the very fabric of our communities. We support the historic places that have survived; we share stories, photos and memories of the people and places that are gone. We mourn the loss of a historic building when it's knocked down to make way for "progress" and celebrate the preservation of a crumbling structure being renovated for another use. We care about who and what went before us and know that sometimes what appears to be lost is really just waiting to be discovered.

BIBLIOGRAPHY

Ancestry.com. "William Rucker in the 1940 Census." https://www.
ancestry.com/1940-census/usa/Ohio/William-Rucker_1683f1.

Anderson, Karl Ricks. *Joseph Smith's Kirtland Eyewitness Accounts.* Salt Lake
City, UT: Deseret Book, 1989.

Associated Press. "Escaped Circus Elephant Captured." February 16, 1998.

Baker, Dane. "Rumrunning on the Great Lakes." *Bar Stool Talk* (blog).
https://barstooltalk.com/2018/04/09/rum-running-on-the-great-lakes/.

Baker, Lindsay. "Where Does the Red Carpet Come From?" BBC,
February 22, 2016. https://www.bbc.com/culture/article/20160222-
where-does-the-red-carpet-come-from.

"Battered Coffin in Cliff at Willoughbeach Recalls Worst Tragedy in
History of Old Erie." Newspaper clipping, July 1910. City of Willowick
archives.

Birding in Ohio. "Mentor Beach Park." https://birding-in-ohio.com/lake-
county/mentor-beach-park/.

Boresz Engelking, Jennifer. *Hidden History of Lake County, Ohio.* Charleston,
SC: The History Press, 2021.

Boyer, Dwight. "That Was Ohio: The Day Fairport Blew." *Plain Dealer*
(Cleveland, OH) *Sunday Magazine,* January 2, 1972.

Brewster Nighman, Lorna. "Glimpses of the Past." *Painesville (OH)
Telegraph,* October 31, 1969.

Bryant, Nelson. "Old Fishing Lures Now Attracting Cash." *Chicago Tribune,*
October 16, 1988. https://www.chicagotribune.com/news/ct-xpm-
1988-10-16-8802080437-story.html.

Cameron, Jim. "Getting There: Historic 20th Century Limited Train Service Remains Unmatched." *Connecticut Post* (Bridgeport, CT), December 3, 2018. https://www.ctpost.com/local/article/Getting-There-Historic-20th-Century-Limited-13424954.php.

Camp, Mark J. *Railroad Depots of Northeast Ohio*. Charleston, SC: Arcadia Publishing, 2007.

Camp Roosevelt Firebird. "The Start of Our Ohio Summer Camp." https://www.camprooseveltfirebird.com/learn-about-camp/about-us/since-1918/.

Canterbury Golf Club. "History." https://www.canterburygc.org/about/history.

Cardwell, Leta D. "History of Kirtland Education." Master's thesis, Purdue University, December 6, 1972.

Carnegie Hero Fund Commission. https://www.carnegiehero.org.

Carousel Organ 79 (April 2019). https://coaa.us/resources/Print-Files/%2379.pdf?fbclid=IwAR08u4tINU52gZPAKDkO3Zhs6hWFhELwj6Jc-Zfw6Ka9FiU_6KI8FhjjlyQ.

Chillicothe (OH) Gazette. "Murder Trial and Ghost Story in Combination." October 19, 1922.

Chojnacki, Linda. "Do You Know the Legend of Squire's Castle?" Cleveland.com. https://www.cleveland.com/our-town/2012/01/do_you_know_the_legend_of_squires_castle.html.

Cinema Treasures. "Skyway Drive-In." http://cinematreasures.org/theaters/18076.

———. "Eastlake Drive-In." http://cinematreasures.org/theaters/6857.

———. "Euclid Avenue Outdoor Theater." http://cinematreasures.org/theaters/6856.

———. "Mentor Twin Drive-In." http://cinematreasures.org/theaters/6885.

City of Mentor. "History of Mentor Timeline." https://cityofmentor.com/wp-content/uploads/History-of-Mentor-Timeline-rev.-2019-1.pdf.

———. "The Mysterious Wreck of the 20th Century Limited." https://cityofmentor.com/the-mysterious-wreck-of-the-20th-century-limited/.

Cleveland 19 News. "Meteotsunami That Ripped through Lake Erie Isn't Uncommon on the Great Lakes." Last updated April 29, 2019. https://www.cleveland19.com/2019/04/30/meteotsunami-that-ripped-through-lake-erie-isnt-uncommon-great-lakes/.

Cleveland (OH) Plain Dealer. "Complete Plans for Country Club—Work on New Willowick Clubhouse to Be Started within Ten Days." September 18, 1910.

Cleveland (OH) Press. "Club Officers Are Elected." September 30, 1910.

———. "Eastlake Dynamites Chagrin River Ice." January 16, 1969.

———. "Enlarges Its Golf Links—Willowick Country Club Will Have Eighteen-Hole Course." May 4, 1913.

———. "Kirtland Mill Will Be Razed." March 26, 1924.

———. "New Club to Have Golf This Year—Willowick Course Will be Ready for Play by Next September." April 23, 1911

———. "Shore Residents Weigh 'Tidal' Wave Damage." June 30, 1952.

———. Untitled clipping. June 23, 1905.

———. "Will Incorporate Club—Property Acquired for New Willowick Country Club on Lake Shore." August 28, 1910.

Cleveland Sailing Association. "84th Annual Falcon Cup Race." https://clevelandsails.com/Portals/2/regattas/Notice_of_Race___84th_Falcon_Cup_2021.pdf?ver=NRThzvDHzMjkiT_5Qd2iGQ%3D%3D.

Curtis, Lillie Tryon. "The Story of Waite Hill—Part I." *Historical Society Quarterly* 20, no. 2 (June 1978).

Dutka, Alan. *Slovenians in Cleveland: A History.* Charleston, SC: The History Press, 2017.

Encyclopedia of Cleveland History. "Harkness, Stephen V." Case Western Reserve University. https://case.edu/ech/articles/h/harkness-stephen-v.

———. "Maritime Disasters." https://case.edu/ech/articles/m/maritime-disasters.

Evening Telegram (Toronto, ON). Nov. 16, 1937.

Fairport Harbor Historical Society. "Edmund Fitzgerald Lost 46-Years Ago, November 10, 1975." *View through the Porthole* 36, no. 4 (November 2021).

———. *Fairport Harbor.* Charleston, SC: Arcadia Publishing, 2003.

———. "*Queen of the West* Artifacts Donated to the Museum." *A View through the Porthole* 36, no. 4 (November 2021).

The Family Parmelee. "Parmly House Hotel." https://thefamilyparmelee.com/a-hotel.html.

"FHS—Fairport History Source." Facebook member page. https://www.facebook.com/groups/257840585938335.

Find a Grave. "Louisa Christiana Breymaier Squire." https://www.findagrave.com/memorial/153878287/louisa-christiana-squire.

———. "Harvey H. Johnson." https://www.findagrave.com/memorial/206676786/harvey-h.-johnson?fbclid=IwAR10iHcJ8gsyKIX8bEdFIOvauCuVsFww7sbPp-aaWPEDTOYpEc5hxRdED_g.

Gast, Ron. "Riley Haskell Minnow Lures." Antique Fishing Lures, Reels & Tackle Information Site. https://luresnreels.com/haskell.html.

Gault, Homer J. *History of Mentor Headlands and Vicinity.* Fairport Harbor, OH: Neal Printing, 1957.

Gestel, Joan. "New Service Sought: Eastlake Cab Company Calls It Quits." *News-Herald* (Willoughby, OH), January 29, 1978.

Gibbons, Timothy J. "Willowick Discovery, Tunnels into Past." *News-Herald* (Willoughby, OH), August 4, 1998.

Hernandis, John. "Willowick—Fix It or Tear It Down Is Order for Old Home." *Cleveland (OH) Press.* April 15, 1965.

Hiscox. "A History of Black Owned Businesses in the U.S." https://www.hiscox.com/blog/history-black-owned-businesses-us.

Holden Forests & Gardens. "History." https://www.holdenarb.org/about/history/.

Holland Dolan, Sheena. "New Group Researching Community History to Launch at Mentor-on-the-Lake Library." *News-Herald* (Willoughby, OH), September 26, 2021. https://www.news-herald.com/2021/09/26/new-group-researching-community-history-to-launch-at-men.

"If You Grew Up in Painesville Ohio You Remember>>>" Facebook member page. https://www.facebook.com/groups/190094721054184.

Independent (Willoughby, OH). November 9, 1883.

———. November 25, 1898.

Kapsch, Joan, Sue Muehlhauser and Kathie Pohl. *Mentor: The First 200 Years.* Mentor, OH: Mentor Bicentennial Committee/Old Mentor Foundation, 1997.

Koile, Wendy. *Legends and Lost Treasure of Northern Ohio.* Charleston, SC: The History Press, 2014.

Lake County Genealogical Society. "Griffith Disaster Burial Ground (Kennedy Farm)." https://www.lcgsohio.org/cemeteries/willoughby-cemeteries/griffith-disaster-burial-ground-kennedy-farm/.

Lake County Historical Society. *Here Is Ohio's Lake County.* Chelsea, MI: Sheridan Books, 2014.

———. *Historical Society Quarterly* 11, no. 1 (February 1969).

———. *Historical Society Quarterly* 30 (June 1988).

"Lake County History Center." Facebook member page. https://www.facebook.com/lakecountyhistory.

Lake County History Center News 63, no. 1 (Spring 2021).

Lake County History Center. "Lake County Railroad Potpourri." http://lakehistorycenter.org/wp-content/uploads/2019/05/LCHS-May-2019.pdf.

————. "Made in Lake County—The Early Titans." http://lakehistorycenter.org/wp-content/uploads/2021/05/May-2021-LCHS7423.pdf.

————. "Summer Nights at the Lake County Drive-Ins." http://lakehistorycenter.org/wp-content/uploads/2021/06/LCHS-Blog-June-2021-DriveIns.pdf.

————. "Willoughby Chandler-Tucker Estates." https://lakehistorycenter.org/willoughby-chandler-tucker-estate/.

Lake Metroparks. "Indian Point Park." http://www.lakemetroparks.com/parks-trails/indian-point-park.

"LeRoy Heritage Association." Facebook member page. https://www.facebook.com/LeroyHeritageAssociation.

Letterpress Commons. "Chandler and Price Oldstyle." https://letterpresscommons.com/press/chandler-price-oldstyle/.

Lippucci, Gale. "Willowick History Project." Willoughby-Eastlake Public Library. https://we247.org/info/local-history/willowick-history-project/.

Lodge, Richard K. "Alluring Auction: Metal Minnow Could Fetch $50,000." *Steuben Courier Advocate* (Bath, NY), October 31, 2007. https://www.steubencourier.com/article/20071031/NEWS/310319967?template=ampart.

Louis Penfield House. "Frank Lloyd Wright and the Penfields." https://www.penfieldhouse.com/about/about.

Lupold, Harry Forrest. *The Latch String Is Out: A Pioneer History of Lake County, Ohio.* Mentor, OH: Lakeland Community College Press, 1974.

"Madison Historical Society, Madison, Ohio." Facebook member page. https://www.facebook.com/HistoricalMadisonOhio.

Major League Fishing. "Antique Lure Sells for World-Record $101,200." https://majorleaguefishing.com/uncategorized/2003-11-18-antique-lure-sells-for-world-record-101-200/.

Mansfield, John Brandt. *History of the Great Lakes: Illustrated.* Chicago, IL: 1899.

Maritime History of the Great Lakes. "G.P. Griffith (Steamboat), 18 Oct 1847." http://images.maritimehistoryofthegreatlakes.ca/28816/data?n=1.

————. "G.P. Griffith (Steamboat), burnt, 17 June 1850." http://images.maritimehistoryofthegreatlakes.ca/47129/data?n=4.

Matowitz, Thomas. City of Mentor. "Hometown Hero Albert Clapp." Nov. 25, 2016. https://cityofmentor.com/hometown-hero-albert-clapp/.

———. *Mentor.* Mount Pleasant, SC: Arcadia Publishing, 2015.

Maxson, Daniel. "Lake County History Grab Bag- part 2/3 The Interurban." Lake County History Center. http://lakehistorycenter.org/wp-content/uploads/2021/12/Dan-Maxson-blog-Nov-2021-Part-2-LC-.pdf.

———. "Lost Lake County Drive-Ins." *Local Lore* (blog).

———. "Lost Stories: Yesterday and Today—The Lake Shore Resorts." *Local Lore* (blog). https://wwwnews-heraldcom.blogspot.com/search?q=lake+resort.

Maxson, Daniel, and Bechel-Esker, Debra L. *Concord Township.* Mount Pleasant, SC: Arcadia Publishing, 2021.

Messenger 1, no. 4. (May 1909).

Meszoros, Mark. "Pulled In by Painesville Past's 'Potato.'" *News-Herald* (Willoughby, OH), November 15, 2009. https://www.news-herald.com/2009/11/15/pulled-in-by-painesville-pasts-potato/.

Michaud, Denise, and the Madison Historical Society. *Madison.* Charleston, SC: Arcadia Publishing, 2010.

National Baseball Hall of Fame. "Nap Lajoie." https://baseballhall.org/hall-of-famers/lajoie-nap.

National Museum of American History. "Vulcan Manufacturing Company Radiator Emblem." https://americanhistory.si.edu/collections/search/object/nmah_840111.

Naughton, James E. *70 Years of Living in Kirtland.* Self-published, Mentor, OH: 2021.

News-Herald (Willoughby, OH). "Closed Library Asks for Use of Trailer." August 23, 1957.

———. "Giant Wave Hits Shoreline Here, Rips Cottages, Boats." June 30, 1952.

———. "Library Closed…Tunnel Gas Threatens Explosion." August 22, 1957.

———. "Pump Gas from Foot Tunnel." August 24, 1957.

———. Untitled clipping. May 6, 1930.

New York Times. "Nap Lajoie Obituary." February 9, 1959.

Ohio History Central. "1882 Lake Erie Mystery Wave." https://ohiohistorycentral.org/w/1882_Lake_Erie_Mystery_Wave.

Olila, Saul. *Hometown Sketches 1796–1936.* Fairport, OH: 1936.

Olin, Saul C. *The Story of Fairport, Ohio—Yesterday, Today, Tomorrow.* Fairport, OH: 1946.

Olito, Frank. "17 Vintage Photos from the Heyday of Drive-In Movie Theaters." Insider, March 25, 2019. https://www.insider.com/vintage-pictures-drive-in-movie-theaters-2019-3#by-1958-there-were-4063-drive-in-theaters-nationwide-5.

O'Neill, Marge Mason. "Yesterday an Airfield—Today, School Sites." *Eastlake News & Views* (newsletter), November 1986.

Orris, Sue, and the Madison Historical Society. *History of the Dock Road Arcola Creek Area—Madison Township, Ohio, 1796–1863.* Madison, OH: Lake County Cooperative Extension Service for the Arcola Creek Study Trip, August 9, 1980.

Otis, Charles Augustus. *Here I Am: A Rambling Account of the Exciting Times of Yesteryear.* Cleveland, OH: Buehler Printcraft, 1951

Painesville (OH) Telegraph. "Concord." October 2, 1879.

———. "The Painesville Mills." May 6, 1886. http://usgenwebsites.org/OHLake/history/pvlmills. html?fbclid=IwAR0E2WUapYkxMpxbhLzUO fsu5iqDmzeWAiVsviC9D39GbjRkYXU8JsizUBg.

PeopleLegacy. "Henry C. Dawson." https://peoplelegacy.com/ng/search?fname=Henry&lname=Dawson&state=OH&city=Willoughby.

"People, Places, and History of Lake County, Ohio." Facebook member page. https://www.facebook.com/groups/1201414853349675.

"Perry Historical Society of Lake County." Facebook member page. https://www.facebook.com/perryhistoricalsociety.

Phillips, Dr. Nancymarie. *The Song of the Shepherdess.* Self-published, 2020.

Platko, Mary. *A Little Bit of Perry History.* Bloomington, IN: iUniverse, 2021.

Pollack, Susan R. "*Edmund Fitzgerald* Tragedy Still Draws Reverence." *Detroit News*, November 5, 2014. https://www.detroitnews.com/story/life/2014/11/04/edmund-fitzgerald-legend-lives/18488647/.

Porello, Rick. *Bombs, Bullets, & Bribes: The True Story of Notorious Jewish Mobster Alex Shondor Birns.* Novelty, OH: Next Hat Press, 2020.

Prusha, Anne B. *A History of Kirtland, Ohio.* Mentor, OH: Lakeland Community College Press, 1982.

Roberts, Tawana. "Drive-Ins in Lake County Gone but Not Forgotten." *News-Herald* (Willoughby, OH), July 8, 2016. https://www.news-herald.com/2016/07/08/drive-ins-in-lake-county-gone-but-not-forgotten/.

Rolf, Eleanor Gaines. *Willoughy Township Schools: The First One Hundred Years, 1829–1929.* Willoughby, OH: Willoughby-Eastlake Board of Education, 1978.

Roots of American Music. "Ohio Heritage Music Project: The Ghost of Frank Lloyd Wright." July 10, 2019. https://podcasts.apple.com/us/podcast/ohio-heritage-music-project-episode-1-ghost-frank-lloyd/id1472367783?i=1000444130549.

Roy, Chris. "Squire's Castle." Cleveland Historical. https://clevelandhistorical.org/items/show/836.

Scott, Michael. "Willoughby's 'Sheep Lady' Found Dead on Her Farm." Cleveland.com, January 8, 2004. https://www.cleveland.com/whateverhappened/2004/01/willoughbys_sheep_lady_found_d.html.

Scranton (PA) Truth. "Exact Cause of the Disaster is in Doubt." June 22, 1905. https://www.newspapers.com/clip/15299772/train-wreck-at-mentor-ohio-in-1905/.

Segall, Grant. "Willoughby-Eastlake Schools Reopen Thursday, Fire-Ravaged Office Will Be Bulldozed." Cleveland.com, March 15, 2017. https://www.cleveland.com/metro/2017/03/willoughby-eastlake_schools_reopen_thursday_fire-ravaged_office_will_be_bulldozed_photos.html.

Shankland, Frank N. "Local Resident Describes Inn, Taverns, Hotels, Where Coaches Stopped in 1800s." Newspaper clipping. Archives of the Little Red Schoolhouse in Willoughby, Ohio.

Shepard, Don. "Girls Friendly Society, Holiday House, Salida Beach." Lake County Ohio GenWeb. Originally published April 1908. http://usgenwebsites.org/OHLake/church/girlshse.html.

Signature Smiles. "The Evolution of Dental Floss." August 15, 2017. https://www.signaturesmilesfamilydentistry.com/blog/evolution-dental-floss/.

Silvi, Lee. "Taubman's [*sic*] Fire. February 20, 1981." *View through the Porthole* 35, no. 1 (February 2020).

Sperry, Kip. *Kirtland Ohio: A Guide to Family History and Historical Services.* Provo, UT: Religious Studies Center, Brigham Young University, 2005.

St. Hubert's Episcopal Church. "About Us." http://www.sthuberts.net/about_us.

Telegraph Republican (Painesville, OH). "A Dog Fireman." September 28, 1909.

Village of Fairport Harbor. "History of Fairport Harbor." https://fairportharbor.org/about/history/.

Weber, Cathi. *Haunted Willoughby.* Charleston, SC: The History Press, 2010.

Wickham, Gertrude Van Rennselaer. *The Pioneer Families of Cleveland 1796–1840.* Evangelical Publishing House, 1914.

Wickliffe Historical Society. *The Lloyd Papers II* 19, no. 1 (Winter 2009).

Williams Brothers. *History of Geauga and Lake Counties, Ohio.* Philadelphia, PA: J.B. Lippincott, 1878.

"Willoughby Historical Society." Facebook member page. https://www.facebook.com/WilloughbyHistoricalSociety.

Willoughby (OH) Independent. "Double Tragedy at the Kingsley Hotel." June 12, 1908.

Willoughby (OH) Republican. "Invitations Out for Opening of the Manakiki Country Club." May 6, 1930.

WKCY Studios. "Fire Destroys Willoughby-Eastlake BOE Building; School Canceled Wednesday." https://www.wkyc.com/article/news/local/lake-county/fire-destroys-willoughby-eastlake-boe-building-school-canceled-wednesday/422335414.

"Wonderful Willoughby, Ohio." Facebook member page. https://www.facebook.com/groups/65083165776.

Worrel, Chris M. "Author Discusses Deadly 1850 Lake Erie Shipping Disaster." Cleveland.com, October 26, 2011. https://www.cleveland.com/euclid/2011/10/author_discusses_deadly_1850_l.html.

ABOUT THE AUTHOR

Jennifer Boresz Engelking is the author of *Hidden History of Lake County, Ohio*. She is an award-winning and regional Emmy–nominated writer who has worked in both print and broadcast journalism. She has been a published writer for about two decades, and her work has been printed in several magazines and newspapers, including the *News-Herald* and *Lake Erie Living*.

Jennifer was a reporter for several years at CBS affiliate stations in Toledo, Ohio, and Erie, Pennsylvania, and more recently has written and coproduced several historical documentaries. She has even been on the big screen in several major motion pictures, including the Tony Scott–directed film *Unstoppable*, in which she plays a reporter.

Jennifer was born and raised in Lake County and enjoys exploring the region's parks and historic sites with her husband and three children. Her website is www.jenniferboresz.com.